Charles J. James
Assistant Professor of German
University of Wisconsin (Madison)

German Verbs
and Essentials
of Grammar

a practical guide
to the mastery of German

PASSPORT BOOKS
a division of *NTC Publishing Group*
Lincolnwood, Illinois USA

1994 Printing

Published by Passport Books, a division of NTC Publishing Group.
© 1988, 1985 by NTC Publishing Group, 4255 West Touhy Avenue,
Lincolnwood (Chicago), Illinois 60646-1975 U.S.A.

3 4 5 6 7 8 9 0 ML 9 8 7 6

Preface

German Verbs and Essentials of Grammar presents to its users the major grammatical concepts of the German language. The book is divided into two parts. In Part I, the major emphasis is placed on the mastery of verbs—their formation and uses, as well as their interconnections with other parts of speech. A chapter devoted to the most common verb prefixes reveals the creative ways in which the German language generates new words. The final chapter of Part I summarizes all the major verb tenses. All the chapters in this section provide numerous examples that highlight the forms and uses of German verbs in a meaningful context. Part II of this book offers concise explanations of the essential parts of German grammar—from the use of the article to rules of sentence formation that are characteristic of the German language. The final chapter of Part II features extensive vocabulary lists, each one related to the activities or objects of everyday life.

Examples illustrating grammar concepts were chosen for their authenticity, their frequency in everyday speech and writing, and their idiomatic quality. Each topic is treated separately, so that users of the book can either work on one topic at a time *or* quickly find the reference needed to help solve a particular difficulty. The table of the principal parts of common German verbs should prove an especially useful reference tool. Such tables provide ample material for creative exercises and extended writing, as well as for oral practice. In addition, the pronunciation section at the beginning of the book provides a helpful key to the main characteristics of the German sound system.

German Verbs and Essentials of Grammar is a valuable handbook that lends itself to a variety of uses. Because its basic approach is to provide simple, concise explanations, it can be used by language learners at all levels of proficiency—from those who have completed one semester's work to those who have attained a high level of mastery but who, from time to time, need a convenient reference to consult on difficult points of grammar. *German Verbs and Essentials of Grammar* can be used for study and review, for individual or group work, as part of a refresher course, or for business, travel, or research.

An excellent complement to this book is *Klett's Modern German and English Dictionary,* which contains an expanded listing of verb forms, guidelines for pronunciation, and abundant examples of the idioms most frequently encountered in contemporary German speech and writing. Other German dictionaries and language references available from Passport Books are listed at the end of this text.

Contents

Part One: German Verbs

Part Two: Essentials of Grammar

Part One:
German Verbs

1. Pronunciation

The Alphabet

The German alphabet contains 26 letters. In addition, there are the three *umlaut* letters *ä, ö,* and *ü,* and the so-called *scharfes s* ("sharp s"), ß. These four letters are not part of the basic alphabet, although they are treated like letters in every other way. Letters of the alphabet are all neuter in gender *(das).*

The symbols between brackets ([ ]) indicate the pronunciation of the German names for the letters as rendered by the International Phonetic Alphabet.

a	[aː]	i	[iː]	q	[kuː]	y	[ʏpsɪlɔn]
b	[beː]	j	[jɔt]	r	[er]	z	[tsɛt]
c	[tseː]	k	[kaː]	s	[ɛs]	ß	[ɛstsɛt]
d	[deː]	l	[ɛl]	t	[teː]	ä	[ɛː]
e	[eː]	m	[ɛm]	u	[uː]	ö	[øː]
f	[ɛf]	n	[ɛn]	v	[faʊ]	ü	[yː]
g	[geː]	o	[oː]	w	[veː]		
h	[haː]	p	[peː]	x	[ɪks]		

[ː]   The previous vowel is long.
[ˈ]   The following syllable is stressed.
[ˌ]   The following syllable has secondary stress (rare).
[ʔ]   The so-called "glottal stop" (rare).
[-]   In a series of syllables represents each individual syllable; in a partial transcription represents the remainder of the word.

Großes A capital A   *kleines a* small a

The English equivalents are given as guidelines to pronunciation, not as exact correspondents. Where no English equivalent is given, the sound and its spelling are close enough in both English and German to cause no significant pronunciation difficulties.

Vowels

[i]	bieten	[ˈbitən]	like English *ee* in *bee*
	zivil	[tsiˈviːl]	
[ɪ]	bitten	[ˈbɪtən]	like English *i* in *bit*
[e]	beten	[ˈbeːtən]	like English *ay* in *bay*
	wehren	[ˈveːrən]	

[ɛ]	betten ['bɛtən]	like English *e* in *bet*
	währen ['vɛːrən]	
[a]	Maat [maːt]	like English *o* in *not*
	wahren ['vaːrən]	
	banal [ba'naːl]	
[o]	Ofen ['ofːən]	like English *oa* in *boat*
	Ozon [o'tsoːn]	
[ɔ]	offen ['ɔfən]	like English *ou* in *bought* but much shorter!
[ø]	Öfen *pl* ['øːfən]	like English *ir* in *girl* but without the *r*
	Höhle ['høːlə]	
[œ]	öffnen ['œfnən]	like German [ø] but shorter
	Hölle ['hœlə]	
[u]	Pute ['puːtə]	like English *oo* in *boot*
	zumute [tsu'muːtə]	
[ʊ]	Putte ['pʊtə]	like English *u* in *put*
	Mutter ['mʊtɐ]	
[y]	Tüte ['tyːtə]	like German *i* and *u* pronounced together
[ʏ]	Hütte [hʏtə]	like German [y] but shorter
[ɐ]	aber ['aːbɐ]	vocalic *r*
	Ruhr [ruːɐ]	
[ə]	beleben [bə'le.bən]	like English *e* in *butter*
[aɪ]	mein [maɪn]	like English *i* in *mine*
[aʊ]	Maus [maʊs]	like English *ou* in *mouse*
[ɔɪ]	neu [nɔɪ]	like English *oy* in *boy*
	Mäuse *pl* ['mɔɪzə]	
[ã]	Balance [ba'lãːs]	like English (French) *an* in *nuance*
[õ]	Bonbon [bõ'bõː]	like French *on* in *bon*
[œ̃]	Parfum [par'fœ̃ː]	like French *um* in *parfum*
[ɛ̃]	Bassin [ba'sɛ̃ː]	like French *in* in *bassin*

Consonants

[b]	Bibel ['biːbəl]	like English *b* in *baby*
[ç]	nicht [nɪçt]	between English *sh* and *k*
	ächten ['ɛçtən]	
[x]	Nacht [naxt]	behind English *k* but with mild friction
	achten ['axtən]	
[d]	doch [dɔx]	like English *d* in *drum*
[f]	Frevel ['freːfəl]	like English *f* in *fifty*
	Vielfalt ['fiːlfalt]	
[g]	gegen [ge:gən]	always like English *g* in *go*
[ʒ]	Genie [ʒe'niː]	like second *g* in English *garage*
	Garage [ga'raːʒə]	
[h]	Hahn [haːn]	like English *h* in *hat*
[j]	jagen ['jaːgən]	always like English *y* in *yes*
[k]	Krieg [kriːk]	like English *k* in *keep*
	Knick [knɪk]	
[l]	lallen ['lalən]	like English *l* in *lily*
	labil [la'biːl]	
[m]	Mumm [mʊm]	like English *m* in *murmur*
[n]	nennen ['nɛnɛn]	like English *n* in *no*

[ŋ]	fangen	[ˈfaŋən]	always like *ng* in English *singer*
	denken	[ˈdɛŋkən]	never like *ng* in English *finger*
[p]	Pappe	[ˈpapə]	like English *p* in *pepper*
[r]	Rohre *pl*	[ˈroːrə]	pronounced off the uvula in some varieties, trilled in others, never like English *r*
[s]	Mars	[mars]	like English *s* in *less*
	küssen	[ˈkʏsən]	
	fließen	[ˈfliːsən]	
[z]	Sense	[ˈzɛnzə]	like English *z* in *zebra*
	sausen	[ˈzauzən]	
[ʃ]	Schau	[ʃau]	like English *sh* in *she*
	stehlen	[ˈʃteːlən]	
	spielen	[ˈʃpiːlən]	
[t]	Tat	[taːt]	like English *t* in *tie*
	Tod	[toːt]	
[ts]	Zoo	[tsoː]	like English *ts* in *recruits*
	Zitze	[tsɪtse]	
[v]	Wein	[vaɪn]	like English *v* in *vivid*

Punctuation Marks

,	das Komma		( )	die runde(n) Klammer (n)
.	der Punkt		[ ]	die eckige(n) Klammer(n)
:	der Doppelpunkt		'	der Apostroph
;	der Strichpunkt		-	der Bindestrich
?	das Fragezeichen		—	der Gedankenstrich
!	das Ausrufungszeichen		" "	die Anführungsstriche

2. Subject Pronouns

Singular			Plural		
1.	**ich**	I	1.	**wir**	we
2.	**du**	you	2.	**ihr**	you
	Sie	you		**Sie**	you
3.	**er**	he, it			
	sie	she, it		**sie**	they
	es	it			
	man	you, they, people, etc.			

Sie is the polite form of "you." It is used with strangers, superiors, professional colleagues, and others not well known to the speaker. *Sie* can be singular or plural in meaning, depending on context.

Herr und Frau Schmidt, können *Sie* es heute bringen?	Mr. and Mrs. Schmidt, can you bring it today?
Frau Eckert, haben *Sie* gerade angerufen?	Mrs. Eckert, did you just call?

Du is the familiar form of "you." Its plural is *ihr*. It is used when speaking to family members, children, close friends, animals, and deities.

Wohnst *du* schon lange hier, Martin?	Have you lived here long, Martin?
Wohnt *ihr* schon lange hier, Kinder?	Have you lived here long, children?

The subject pronoun *du* is also used pejoratively, when the speaker wishes to show superiority or contempt towards the person to whom he or she is speaking.

Du Feigling!	You coward!

Man corresponds to the English "one," "they," "people," or "you" when it is used without reference to a particular individual. It is very common in German, especially when the speaker wishes to describe an activity without indicating who is performing the activity.

Man *sagt,*...	They say,...
Man *sieht hier*...	You see here...
Man *hat behauptet,*...	It has been claimed,...

3. Present Tense— Regular Verbs

Infinitives

All German verbs have an infinitive ending in -*(e)n*. This is the form found in dictionaries.

ruf*en*   to call   **arbeit*en***   to work
schlaf*en*   to sleep

The infinitive without the ending -*(e)n* is called the *stem*. Endings added to the stem indicate person, number, tense, and mood.

ruf*en*	**er ruf*t***	he calls
schlaf*en*	**sie schlaf*en***	they sleep
arbeit*en*	**ich arbeite*te***	I worked

The present tense expresses an ongoing action, general state, or habitual activity. It corresponds to all three English present tenses, as in

I write letters.
I am writing a letter now.
I do write letters well!

Forming the Present Tense

The present tense is formed by adding the following number and person endings to the stem.

	Singular				Plural	
1.	**ich**	*-e*		1.	**wir**	*-en*
2.	**du**	*-st*		2.	**ihr**	*-t*
	Sie	*-en*			**Sie**	*-en*
3.	**man**	*-t*		3.	**sie**	*-en*

machen, to do
I do, do do, am doing, you do, etc.

Singular		Plural	
1. **ich mache**	I do	1. **wir machen**	we do
2. **du machst**	you do	2. **ihr macht**	you do
Sie machen	you do	**Sie machen**	you do
3. **er macht**	it, he does	3. **sie machen**	they do
sie macht	it, she does		
es macht	it does		
man macht	people do		

Was machst du?	What are you doing?
Ich mache meine Hausaufgabe.	I am doing my homework.
Er macht alles falsch!	He does everything wrong!
So (et)was macht man hier nicht!	You don't do that sort of thing here!

Sample Verbs Conjugated in the Present Tense like *machen*

brauchen to need	**lernen** to learn
bringen to bring	**lieben** to love
denken to think	**liegen** to lie, to recline
drucken to print	**rufen** to call someone
drücken to press, to push	**sagen** to say
fragen to ask someone	**schicken** to send
führen to lead, to guide	**singen** to sing
gehen to go	**sitzen** to sit
heißen to be called	**spielen** to play
holen to fetch, to get something	**stehen** to stand
horen to hear, to listen	**stellen** to put something into a
kaufen to buy	vertical position
kennen to know somebody	**suchen** to look for
kochen to cook, to boil	**trinken** to drink
kommen to come	**wohnen** to live somewhere
lachen to laugh	**zeigen** to show
leben to live, to be alive	
legen to put something into a	
horizontal position	

Most verbs in German form their present tense like the verbs above.

Verb Stems ending in -t(-), -d(-), or -gn(-)

Verbs whose stem ends in *-t*(-), *-d*(-), *-d*(-) or *-gn*(-) usually add an *-e*(-) before attaching the endings *-st* and *-t*.

arbeiten, to work

I work, do work, am working, etc.

Singular
1. **ich arbeite**   I work
2. **du arbeitest**   you work
   Sie arbeiten   you work
3. **er arbeitet**   he works
   sie arbeitet   she works
   es arbeitet   it works
   man arbeitet   people work

Plural
1. **wir arbeiten**   we work
2. **ihr arbeitet**   you work
   Sie arbeiten   you work
3. **sie arbeiten**   they work

Ich arbeite Tag und Nacht.
Wo arbeitet Ihre Frau?
Sie arbeitet bei einer Bank.

I work day and night.
Where does your wife work?
She works at a bank.

Sample Verbs Conjugated in the Present Tense like *arbeiten*

antworten   to answer
bieten   to offer
binden   to tie
bitten   to request, to ask for
finden   to find
heiraten   to marry
leiden   to suffer

leisten   to accomplish
leiten   to direct
melden   to report in
reden   to give a speech
regnen   to rain
schneiden   to cut
toten   to kill

Stem-Vowel Change Verbs

A number of common verbs change the vowel in their stem in the second person singular informal (*du*) and third person singular forms (*er, sie,* or *man*). The pattern of change is as follows:

a   becomes   **ä**
au   becomes   **äu**
e   becomes   **ie** or **i**
o   becomes   **ö**

Verbs with *u* in the stem do not undergo this change.

geben, to give

I give, do give, am giving, etc.

Singular
1. **ich gebe**   I give
2. **du gibst**   you give
   Sie geben   you give
3. **er gibt**   he gives
   sie gibt   she gives
   es gibt   it gives
   man gibt   people give

Plural
1. **wir geben**   we give
2. **ihr gebt**   you give
   Sie geben   you give
3. **sie geben**   they give

Gibst du mir das Geld?			Are you giving me the money?		
Er gibt dir das Geld.			He gives you the money.		

sehen, to see
I see, do see, am seeing, etc.

Singular			Plural		
1. **ich sehe**	I see		1. **wir sehen**	we see	
2. **du siehst**	you see		2. **ihr seht**	you see	
Sie sehen	you see		**Sie sehen**	you see	
3. **er sieht**	he sees		3. **sie sehen**	they see	
sie sieht	she sees				
es sieht	it sees				
man sieht	people see				

Ich sehe, was du nicht siehst.	I see what you don't see.
Man sieht die Sterne mit dem bloßen Augen.	You (can) see the stars with the naked eye.

tragen, to wear, to carry
I wear, carry, am wearing, am carrying, etc.

Singular			Plural		
1. **ich trage**	I wear		1. **wir tragen**	we wear	
2. **du trägst**	you wear		2. **ihr tragt**	you wear	
Sie tragen	you wear		**Sie tragen**	you wear	
3. **er trägt**	he wears		3. **sie tragen**	they wear	
sie trägt	she wears				
es trägt	it wears				
man trägt	people wear				

Ein Deutscher trägt selten Lederhosen.	A German rarely wears *Lederhosen.*
Trägst du deine neue Uhr?	Are you wearing your new watch?
Ein Gepäckträger trägt Gepäck.	A porter carries baggage.

Sample Verbs with a Stem-Vowel Change

brechen (*bricht*) to break	**schlafen (*schläft*)** to sleep
essen (*ißt*) to eat	**schlagen (*schlägt*)** to hit
fahren (*fährt*) to drive, to go	**sterben (*stirbt*)** to die
fallen (*fällt*) to fall	**stossen (*stößt*)** to push
empfehlen (*empfiehlt*) to recommend	**treten (*tritt*)** to step
halten (*hält*) to hold	**vergessen (*vergißt*)** to forget
laden (*lädt*) to load	**wachsen (*wächst*)** to grow
laufen (*läuft*) to walk, to run	**waschen (*wäscht*)** to wash
lesen (*liest*) to read	

Negative Form

To form a negative verb statement, place *nicht* after the verb.

Es regnet *nicht.*	It does not rain./It is not raining.
Wir antworten *nicht.*	We do not answer./We are not answering.
Das Auto geht *nicht.*	The car does not work./The car isn't working.

See Chapter 28, **Negatives,** for a further discussion of the placement of *nicht*, as well as the use of other negatives, such as *kein, niemand, nie,* and *nichts.*

Interrogative Form

To form a question, simply place the subject after the verb. German does not use a form such as "do" or "does."

Sprechen Sie Deutsch?	Do you speak German?/Are you speaking German?
Schreibt dein Freund oft?	Does your friend write often?
Haben Sie Zeit?	Do you have time?

4. Present Tense— Irregular Verbs

1. There is only one genuinely irregular verb in German, *sein*.

sein, to be
I am, you are, it is, etc.

Singular		Plural	
1. **ich bin**	I am	1. **wir sind**	we are
2. **du bist**	you are	2. **ihr seid**	you are
3. **man ist***	one is	3. **sie sind***	they are

Ich bin Berliner.	I am a Berliner.
Wir sind Amerikaner.	We are Americans.
Ihr seid aber lieb.	You are really nice.
Sie sind kindisch.	You (or they) are childish.

2. Three other very common verbs have forms which are slightly irregular, which is why they are listed here.

haben, to have
I have, you have, he has, etc.

Singular		Plural	
1. **ich habe**	I have	1. **wir haben**	we have
2. **du hast**	you have	2. **ihr habt**	you have
3. **man hat***	one has	3. **sie haben***	they have

Ich habe ein Buch.	I have a book.
Man hat selten Zeit.	You rarely have time.
Ihr habt recht.	You are (*lit.* have) right.

* Note: From now on the *Sie* ("you") forms of verbs will not be listed separately since they are *exactly* the same as the third person plural form of *sie*. Also, the *er, sie, es* ("he," "she," "it") forms will be illustrated by the pronoun *man* hereafter.

wissen, to know (a fact)
I know, you know, she knows, etc.

Singular
1. **ich weiß**   I know
2. **du weißt**   you know
3. **man weiß**   one knows

Plural
1. **wir wissen**   we know
2. **ihr wißt**   you know
3. **sie wissen**   they know

Wissen Sie, wer ich bin?
Nein, ich weiß nicht, wer Sie sind!
Viele wissen, was Sie nicht wissen.

Do you know who I am?
No, I don't know who you are!
Many (people) know, what you don't know.

werden, to become, to get, to turn, to change
I become, you become, they become, etc.

Singular
1. **ich werde**   I become
2. **du wirst**   you become
3. **man wird**   one becomes

Plural
1. **wir werden**   we become
2. **ihr werdet**   you become
3. **sie werden**   they become

Das Wetter wird besser.
Ich werde älter.
Ihr Gesicht wird grün.
Ich werde langsam ungeduldig!

The weather is getting better.
I am getting older.
Her (your, their) face is turning green.
I am slowly becoming impatient!

5. Present Tense— Modal Verbs

Modal verbs, also called *modal auxiliaries* (German *Modalverben*), express the ideas of permission, obligation, etc. Their plural forms are regular. Their singular forms, however, exhibit certain irregularities.

können, to be able to
I can, am able to, etc.

Singular
1. **ich kann**
2. **du kannst**
3. **man kann**

Plural
1. **wir können**
2. **ihr könnt**
3. **sie können**

sollen, to be supposed to
I should, ought to, am supposed to, etc.

Singular
1. **ich soll**
2. **du sollst**
3. **man soll**

Plural
1. **wir sollen**
2. **ihr sollt**
3. **sie sollen**

müssen, to have to
I must, have to, am obliged to, etc.

Singular
1. **ich muß**
2. **du mußt**
3. **man muß**

Plural
1. **wir müssen**
2. **ihr müßt**
3. **sie müssen**

wollen, to want to
I want to, you want to, etc.

Singular
1. **ich will**
2. **du willst**
3. **man will**

Plural
1. **wir wollen**
2. **ihr wollt**
3. **sie wollen**

dürfen, to be allowed to
I may, am allowed, have permission to, etc.

Singular	Plural
1. ich darf	1. wir dürfen
2. du darfst	2. ihr dürft
3. man darf	3. sie dürfen

mögen, to like (to)
I like (to), etc.

Singular	Plural
1. ich mag	1. wir mögen
2. du magst	2. ihr mögt
3. man mag	3. sie mögen

Modals are used with the infinitive of a verb that expresses the main idea of a clause or sentence. The infinitive stands at the end of the clause or sentence in question.

Ich schreibe Briefe.	I write letters.
Ich muß Briefe schreiben.	I have to write letters./I must write letters.
Er geht jetzt nach Hause.	He is going home now.
Er will jetzt nach Hause gehen.	He wants to go home now.
Wir besuchen den Gefangenen.	We are visiting the prisoner.
Wir dürfen den Gefangenen besuchen.	We are allowed to visit the prisoner.

6. Future

1. The future is expressed in German in two ways. First of all, it is expressed by the present tense with appropriate time markers.

Ich komme *morgen.*   I'll come tomorrow.
Wir fahren *nächste Woche* **nach**   We'll be going to Australia next week.
   Australien.
Er bringt es *gleich zurück.*   He'll bring it right back.

2. Secondly, there is a future tense that is formed by using the present tense of *werden* plus the infinitive of the verb in question. Note that *werden* operates exactly like a modal auxiliary.

machen to do, to make

ich *werde*...**machen**	I will do	wir *werden*...**machen**	we will do
du *wirst*...**machen**	you will do	ihr *werdet*...**machen**	you will do
man *wird*...**machen**	people will do	sie *werden*...**machen**	they will do

Ich werde morgen kommen.   I'll come tomorrow.
Wir werden nächste Woche nach   We'll be going to Australia next week.
   Australien fahren.
Er wird es gleich zurückbringen. He'll bring it right back.

The future tense is not used as often in German as it is in English.

7. Preterite (Simple Past) Tense—Weak Verbs

German verbs have two sets of past tense forms: the preterite (or simple past) and the present perfect. For all practical purposes their meaning is the same. Both sets of past tense forms have all the meanings found in the English verb forms "I wrote," "I was writing," "I have written," or "I did write."

Preterite:	**Ich schrieb.**	I wrote.
Present Perfect:	**Ich habe geschrieben.**	I was writing.
		I did write.
		I have written.

It is possible to find *both* past tense forms in the same text or conversation for no apparent reason other than personal, regional, or stylistic preference.

Formation of the Preterite

There are two large groups of verbs based on the formation of their preterite tense forms. The groups are frequently labeled *weak* and *strong*. These labels are interesting only from a historical point of view.

Verbs like *machen* are weak verbs. To form their preterite, simply take the stem, add *-te* and then attach the following endings:

ich	—	**wir**	*-n*
du	*-st*	**ihr**	*-t*
man	—	**sie**	*-n*

machen, to do, to make
I did, was doing, did do, have done, etc.

ich mach*te*	I did	**wir mach***ten*	we did
du mach*test*	you did	**ihr mach***tet*	you did
man mach*te*	people did	**sie mach***ten*	they did

Weak verbs are sometimes also called *regular verbs*.

Sample Verbs Conjugated in the Preterite Tense like *machen/machte*.

Infinitive		Preterite	
bauen	to build	**baute**	built
brauchen	to need	**brauchte**	needed
dauern	to last	**dauerte**	lasted
decken	to cover	**deckte**	covered
drücken	to press	**drückte**	pressed
fragen	to ask	**fragte**	asked
führen	to lead	**führte**	led
holen	to fetch	**holte**	fetched
hören	to hear	**hörte**	heard
kaufen	to buy	**kaufte**	bought
kochen	to cook	**kochte**	cooked
lachen	to laugh	**lachte**	laughed
lächeln	to smile	**lächelte**	smiled
lernen	to learn	**lernte**	learned
lieben	to love	**liebte**	loved
schauen	to look at	**schaute**	looked at
schicken	to send	**schickte**	sent
setzen	to set	**setzte**	set
spielen	to play	**spielte**	played
stören	to disturb	**störte**	disturbed
suchen	to look for	**suchte**	looked for
zeigen	to show	**zeigte**	showed

8. Preterite Tense— Strong Verbs

Verbs like *sehen* are *strong* verbs. They require a change in the stem vowel that is not always predictable. The same thing often happens in English: "see"— "saw," "do"—"did," "come"—"came," "go"—"went," "be"—"was," etc. The preterite (simple past) tense endings for strong verbs are the same as those for weak verbs such as *machen*.

ich	—	wir	*-en*
du	*-st*	ihr	*-t*
man	—	sie	*-en*

sehen, to see
I saw, was seeing, did see, have seen, etc.

ich sah	wir sahen
du sahst	ihr saht
man sah	sie sahen

Ich sah sie gestern	I saw her yesterday.
Wir sahen den Film nicht.	We didn't see the film.

As with English irregular verbs, the vowel changes for strong verbs have to be memorized.

Sample Verbs Conjugated in the Preterite Tense like *sehen/sah*.

Infinitive		Preterite	
brechen	to break	brach	broke
fahren	to drive	fuhr	drove
fallen	to fall	fiel	fell
fangen	to catch	fing	caught
geben	to give	gab	gave
gehen	to go	ging	went
helfen	to help	half	helped
kommen	to come	kam	came
laufen	to run	lief	ran
liegen	to lie	lag	lay
lügen	to tell a lie	log	lied
nehmen	to take	nahm	took
pfeiffen	to whistle	pfiff	whistled

reissen	to tear	**riß**	tore
riechen	to smell	**roch**	smelled
rufen	to call	**rief**	called
schlafen	to sleep	**schlief**	slept
schlagen	to hit	**schlug**	hit
schreiben	to write	**schrieb**	wrote
singen	to sing	**sang**	sang
sprechen	to speak	**sprach**	spoke
stehen	to stand	**stand**	stood
steigen	to climb	**stieg**	climbed
sterben	to die	**starb**	died
tragen	to wear	**trug**	wore
trinken	to drink	**trank**	drank
werfen	to throw	**warf**	threw
ziehen	to pull	**zog**	pulled

Sein, Haben, and Werden

The verbs *sein, haben,* and *werden* have predictable preterite forms, but are listed here as further examples of the formation of the preterite.

sein, to be
I was, was being, have been, etc.

ich war	**wir waren**
du warst	**ihr wart**
man war	**sie waren**

Warst du gestern zu Hause?	Were you home yesterday?
Nein, ich war bei meiner Tante.	No, I was visiting (at) my aunt.

haben, to have
I had, was having, did have, have had, etc.

ich hatte	**wir hatten**
du hattest	**ihr hattet**
man hatte	**sie hatten**

Ich hatte einmal einen Hund.	I once had a dog.
Meine Schwester und ich hatten ihn sehr gern.	My sister and I liked him very much (*lit.* had him very gladly).

werden, to become
I became, was becoming, did become, have become, etc.

ich wurde	**wir wurden**
du wurdest	**ihr wurdet**
man wurde	**sie wurden**

Was wurden Ihre Eltern?	What did your parents become?
Meine Mutter wurde Ärztin und mein Vater wurde Pilot.	My mother became a physician and my father became a pilot.

9. Preterite Tense—Modal Verbs and Mixed Verbs

The Preterite of Modal Verbs

Some modal verbs have an irregular stem in the preterite, but *all* modals have a regular (*-te*) past tense marker. Note that the preterite (simple past) tense endings for modals are the same as those for weaker verbs (see page 17).

können, to be able to
I was able to, could, you were able to, you could, etc.

ich konnte	wir konnten
du konntest	ihr konntet
man konnte	sie konnten

Ich konnte es kaum glauben!	I could hardly believe it!
Wir konnten es uns nicht leisten.	We couldn't afford it.
Das konnte man klar sehen.	You could see that clearly.

sollen, to be supposed to
I was supposed to, ought to have (-ed), etc.

ich sollte	wir sollten
du solltest	ihr solltet
man sollte	sie sollten

Wir sollten gestern um die Zeit kommen.	We were supposed to come at that time yesterday.
Du solltest das wirklich sehen.	You really should have seen that.

müssen, to have to
I had to, was obliged to, etc.

ich mußte	wir mußten
du mußtest	ihr mußtet
man mußte	sie mußten

Ich mußte das machen.	I had to do that.
Wir mußten die Aufgabe nicht* machen.	We did not have to do the assignment.

*Note: *Nicht müssen* does <u>not</u> mean "must not."

wollen, to want to
I wanted to, you wanted to, etc.

ich wollte	wir wollten
du wolltest	ihr wolltet
man wollte	sie wollten

Du wolltest es mir schon lange sagen, nicht wahr?	You have wanted to tell me that for a long time, haven't you?
Ich wollte die Nachricht nicht glauben.	I didn't want to believe the report.
Wir wollten auf den Eiffel-Turm steigen.	We wanted to climb (up) the Eiffel Tower.

dürfen, to be allowed to
I was allowed to, had permission to, etc.

ich durfte	wir durften
du durftest	ihr durftet
man durfte	sie durften

Wir wollten ins Kino gehen, aber wir durften nicht.	We wanted to go to the movies, but we were not allowed to.
Ich durfte nicht zu Hause bleiben.	I was not allowed to stay home.

mögen, to like (to)
I liked to, you liked to, etc.

ich mochte	wir mochten
du mochtest	ihr mochtet
man mochte	sie mochten

Ich mochte die Farbe nicht.	I didn't like the color.
Sie mochten den Krimi im Fernsehen.	They liked the mystery film on television.

The Preterite of Mixed Verbs

In addition to the modal verbs, there are a number of common verbs, called *mixed verbs,* that form their preterite by changing the stem and adding -*te.* These verbs are *bringen, kennen, denken, rennen,* and *wissen. Wissen* is the most common of the mixed verbs and serves as a model for the others.

wissen, to know (a fact)
I knew, did know, have known, etc.

ich wußte	wir wußten
du wußtest	ihr wußtet
man wußte	sie wußten

Ich wußte es doch!	I did (too) know that!
Wir wußten nicht, wie lange es dauern sollte.	We didn't know how long it was supposed to last.

10. Past Participles and the Present Perfect Tense

1. German has three perfect tenses: the present perfect *(Perfekt)*, past perfect *(Plusquamperfekt)*, and future perfect *(Futurum Perfekt)*. The perfect tenses are also called "compound tenses." Only the present perfect is used extensively.

2. The present perfect is formed by using the past participle plus the present tense of either *haben* or *sein*.

Er *hat* **in Paris** *gewohnt.*　　　He lived in Paris.
Wir *sind* **ins Kino** *gegangen.*　　We went to the movies.

The past participle of weak verbs is formed by taking the stem of the verb, adding -*t* to the end, and prefixing *ge-*.

machen to do　　　　　　　　*gemacht* done

Other verbs like *machen* form their past participle exactly the same way. Here are some of the most common.

Infinitive		Past Participle	
bauen	to build	**gebaut**	built
decken	to cover	**gedeckt**	covered
fragen	to ask	**gefragt**	asked
hören	to hear	**gehört**	heard
kaufen	to buy	**gekauft**	bought
lachen	to laugh	**gelacht**	laughed
lernen	to learn	**gelernt**	learned
lieben	to love	**geliebt**	loved
sagen	to say, tell	**gesagt**	said, told
spielen	to play	**gespielt**	played
suchen	to look for	**gesucht**	looked for
zeigen	to show	**gezeigt**	showed

3. Verbs such as *antworten,* which add an *-e*(-) before attaching the endings *-st* and *-t* in the present, add an *-e*(-) before attaching the *-t* of the past participle.

antworten   to answer   **geantwort*et***   answered

Infinitive	Past Participle
arbeiten to work	**gearbeitet** worked
heiraten to get married	**geheiratet** got married
leisten to accomplish	**geleistet** accomplished
leiten to conduct	**geleitet** conducted
reden to give a speech	**geredet** given a speech
regnen to rain	**geregnet** rained
töten to kill	**getötet** killed

4. Strong verbs like *brechen* usually add *-en* instead of *-t* to the end of the past participle. In many strong verbs, there is also a change in the stem vowel.

brechen   to break   **gebroch*en***   broken

Some other past participles of strong verbs include:

Infinitive	Past Participle
binden to tie	**gebunden** tied
bleiben to stay	**geblieben** stayed
finden to find	**gefunden** found
geben to give	**gegeben** given
lesen to read	**gelesen** read
rufen to call	**gerufen** called
werden to become	**geworden** become

5. The following past participles have certain irregularities in their formation, but also end in *-en* and begin with *ge-:*

Infinitive	Past Participle
essen to eat	**gegessen** eaten
gehen to go	**gegangen** gone
nehmen to take	**genommen** taken
sein to be	**gewesen** been
sitzen to sit	**gesessen** sat
stehen to stand	**gestanden** stood

Past Participles without *ge-*

All verbs whose infinitive ends in *-ieren* form the past participle without the *ge-* prefix. Instead, they take the *-t* ending common to the past participles of weak verbs, which they all are.

Infinitive		Past Participle	
delegieren	to delegate	**delegiert**	delegated
interessieren	to interest	**interessiert**	interested
marschieren	to march	**marschiert**	marched
qualifizieren	to qualify	**qualifiziert**	qualified
regieren	to govern	**regiert**	governed
studieren	to study	**studiert**	studied

Note: All verbs ending in *-ieren* are weak verbs and form all their tenses according to the pattern of verbs such as *machen*.

Past Participles with Prefixes

1. Certain verb prefixes "preempt" the *ge-* participial prefix. The meanings and uses of these prefixes will be discussed in Chapter 12, **Verb Prefixes**. The prefixes in question are: *be-, emp-, ent-, er-, ge-, ver-,* and *zer-*. Examples include:

Infinitive		Past Participle	
besuchen	to visit	**besucht**	visited
empfehlen	to recommend	**empfohlen**	recommended
erleben	to experience	**erlebt**	experienced
gefallen	to please	**gefallen**	pleased
vergessen	to forget	**vergessen**	forgotten
zerstören	to destroy	**zerstört**	destroyed

2. Sometimes the following prefixes also override the *ge-* prefix: *durch-, um-, unter-,* and *über-*.

Infinitive		Past Participle	
durchsuchen	to search	**durchsucht**	searched
übersetzen	to translate	**übersetzt**	translated
umschreiben	to transcribe	**umschrieben**	transcribed
unterschreiben	to sign	**unterschrieben**	signed

3. Whether or not the participle will end in *-t* or *-en* depends upon the verb from which it is derived. If the verb with the prefix is taken from a weak verb, it will end in *-t*.

Infinitive		Past Participle	
*be*stellen	to order	**bestellt**	ordered
*ent*setzen	to horrify	**entsetzt**	horrified
*ver*suchen	to try	**versucht**	tried

4. If the verb is taken from a strong verb, it will end in *-en*.

Infinitive		Past Participle	
*be*stehen	to pass	**bestanden**	passed (a test)
*er*finden	to invent	**erfunden**	invented
*ver*stehen	to understand	**verstanden**	understood

Forming the Present Perfect

The present perfect tense is usually formed by using the appropriate present tense form of *haben* and placing the past participle at the end of the clause or sentence.

Hast **du das Buch** *gekauft?*	Have you bought the book?
Ja, und ich *habe* **das Buch auch** *gelesen.*	Yes, and I have also read the book.
Habt **ihr den Film** *gesehen?*	Have you (all) seen the movie?
Ja, und wir *haben* **den Film sehr lustig** *gefunden.*	Yes, and we found the movie very funny.
Haben **die Arbeiter die Brücke** *errichtet?*	Have the workers erected the bridge?
Ja, aber der Chef *hat* **die Arbeit nicht** *genehmigt.*	Yes, but the boss did not approve the work.

Present Perfect with Modals

1. The modal verbs have "true" past participles. However, they are used only when they are "full" verbs, that is, when they are used without an infinitive.

Ich mag Leber nicht und habe sie nie *gemocht.*	I do not like liver and have never liked it.
Wir haben nicht *gewollt,* **daß es zu einem Unfall kommen sollte.**	We didn't want it to come to an accident.
Du kannst nicht tanzen und hast es nie *gekonnt.*	You cannot dance and never have been able to.

2. Otherwise, the infinitive is used where a past participle would be expected. It is placed after the infinitive of the main idea in the sentence.

Present:	**Ich kann schreiben.**	I can write.
Preterite:	**Ich konnte schreiben.**	I was able to write.
Present Perfect:	**Ich** *habe* **schreiben** *können.*	I have been able to write./ I was able to write.
Present:	**Du darfst gehen.**	You may go.
Preterite:	**Du dürftest gehen.**	You were allowed to go.
Present Perfect:	**Du** *hast* **gehen** *dürfen.*	You have been allowed to go./ You were allowed to go.

Note: The modals *all* take *haben* in the present perfect.

3. In the following list, the "true" past participles are given in parentheses:

können	to be able to	**(gekonnt) können**	been able to
dürfen	to be allowed to	**(gedurft) dürfen**	been allowed to
sollen	to be supposed to	**(gesollt) sollen**	been supposed to
müssen	to be obligated to	**(gemußt) müssen**	been obligated to
wollen	to want	**(gewollt) wollen**	wanted
mögen	to like (to)	**(gemocht) mögen**	liked (to)

The Present Perfect Tense with *sein*

A number of common verbs do not use the auxiliary verb *haben* to form their perfect tenses. Instead they use the corresponding forms of *sein*. Most are verbs of motion or being, including *sein* itself. Most of them, in addition, happen to be strong verbs as well.

Ist Herr Braun zu Hause geblieben?	Did Mr. Braun stay at home?
Bist du in die Stadt gefahren?	Did you drive into the city?

Verbs that commonly use *sein* in compound tenses include:

Infinitive		Present Perfect (third person singular)	
bleiben	to stay	**ist geblieben**	stayed
fahren	to go by vehicle	**ist gefahren**	gone by vehicle
fallen	to fall	**ist gefallen**	fallen
fliessen	to flow	**ist geflossen**	flowed
gehen	to go	**ist gegangen**	gone
kommen	to come	**ist gekommen**	come
reisen	to travel	**ist gereist**	traveled
sein	to be	**ist gewesen**	been
steigen	to climb	**ist gestiegen**	climbed
sterben	to die	**ist gestorben**	died
werden	to become	**ist geworden**	become

11. Other Perfect Tenses

The Past Perfect Tense

1. The past perfect is formed exactly like the present perfect except that the appropriate preterite form of *haben* or *sein* is used.

Ich *hatte* das Buch *gelesen.*	I had read the book.
Wir *hatten* den Film gesehen.	We had seen the movie.
Wir *waren* schon *gekommen.*	We had already come.

2. Usually the past perfect is used with one or more other past tenses, since it indicates an activity that occurred before some other activity in the past. The use of the past perfect is as rare in German as it is in English.

Wir haben den Film gesehen, erst nachdem wir den Roman gelesen hatten.	We saw the film only after we had read the novel.
Es hat zu regnen angefangen, nachdem er angekommen war.	It started to rain, after he had arrived.

The Future Perfect Tense

1. The future perfect is formed by using the present tense of *werden* plus the past participle with either *haben* or *sein* at the end of the clause, depending on the verb in question. Sentences in the future perfect in both English and German frequently contain a time expression such as *bis...* ("by...").

Ich werde das Buch bis Montag gelesen haben.	I will have read the book by Monday.
Du wirst den Bericht bis dahin geschrieben haben.	You will have written the report by then.
Er wird bis nächstes Jahr umgezogen sein.	He will have moved by next year.

2. German has a somewhat unusual use for its future perfect. Combined with the adverb *wohl* ("probably"), the future perfect refers to an event that *has probably already taken place,* although the speaker is not sure whether or not this is true.

Mein Sohn wird die Hausaufgaben *wohl* **gemacht haben.**	My son has (probably) already done his homework.
Die Schriftstellerin wird den neuen Roman *wohl* **geschrieben haben.**	The author has (probably) already written her new novel.

12. Verb Prefixes

German verbs have a number of prefixes that change their meaning, just as the prefixes "re-," "en-," and "ex-" change the English word "act" to produce "react," "enact," and "exact." There are two kinds of prefixes in German: separable and inseparable.

Separable Prefixes

1. Separable prefixes are usually removed from the present and preterite tense and placed at the end of the sentence or clause.

anfangen	to begin
Die Stunde fängt um 7.00 Uhr *an.*	The (class) hour begins at 7:00 o'clock.
aufmachen	to open
Der Lehrer machte das Buch *auf.*	The teacher opened the book.
zumachen	to close
Der Lehrer machte das Buch *zu.*	The teacher closed the book.

The most common separable prefixes in German have certain basic meanings that color the meaning of the verb to which they are attached.

ab-	away from, starting from, down from	*ein-*	into
an-	beginning	*her-*	from
auf-	upwards, opening	*hin-*	toward
aus-	out of	*nach-*	afterward, following upon
bei-	attending	*vor-*	in front of, beforehand
durch-	through	*zu-*	closing, adding to
		zurück-	back, returning

2. There are dozens of other separable verb prefixes. Historically many of these are formed from direct objects, such as

*teil***nehmen** to participate (*lit.* "to take part")
*statt***finden** to take place (*lit.* "to find place")
*stand***halten** to stand firm

or adverbs, such as

*fern*sehen   to watch television (*lit.* "to see far")
*fort*dauern   to continue without interruption
*fest*halten   to hold on (*lit.* "to hold firm")
*los*fahren   to start off

or other verbs, such as

*stehen*bleiben   to stop, to come to a stop (*lit.* "to remain standing")
*kennen*lernen   to become acquainted with (*lit.* "to learn to know")

or old prepositional phrases, such as

*abhanden*kommen   to become lost
*imstande*sein   to be able to
*zurecht*kommen   to fit in, to get along

3. By far the largest cohesive set of separable prefixes is formed with the two words *hin-* and *her-*. *Hin-* implies motion towards a point of interest; *her-* implies motion from a point of interest. Some representatives of the *hin-/her-* family are:

hinein-	go into	*herauf-*	come upstairs
herein-	come into	*hinauf-*	go upstairs
	Herein! = "Come in!"	*herunter-*	come downstairs
hinaus-	go out into	*hinunter-*	go downstairs
heraus-	come out into		

4. A number of verbs generate entire "families" of related verbs produced from the addition of separable (and inseparable) prefixes. Take, for example, *ziehen,* which has the basic meaning of "to pull" or "to draw (out)." Adding some of the prefixes listed earlier yields the following:

ziehen to pull		*um***ziehen** to change clothing	
*ab***ziehen** to run off a print		*zurück***ziehen** to move (pull) back	
*an***ziehen** to dress, to put on clothing		*vor***ziehen** to prefer	
*auf***ziehen** to wind up, to pull up			

Note: Many of the above prefixes look like prepositions. They are, however, part of their respective verbs. This can give rise to situations in which a prefix and its preposition look-alike can appear in the same sentence.

Er *stieg* **aus dem Zug aus.**	He got off (out of) the train.
Passen **Sie auf die Stufe** *auf!*	Watch out for the step!
Wir *fangen* **am** (= **an dem**) **Montag** *an.*	We are beginning on Monday.

Inseparable Prefixes

Inseparable prefixes are never removed from their verb forms. In fact, they even replace the *ge-* of the past participle. (See Chapter 10.) The inseparable prefixes also convey meaning, but the meanings are less tangible than those of separable prefixes.

be-   makes a verb transitive, that is, the verb takes an object
         kommen   to come
         *be*kommen   to get, obtain, receive (not "become")

         gehen   to go
         *be*gehen   to commit

emp-   (only three verbs have this prefix)
         fangen   to catch
         *emp*fangen   to receive

         fehlen   to be missing
         *emp*fehlen   to recommend

         finden   to find
         *emp*finden   to be sensitive to

ent-   away from, escape, removal
         nehmen   to take
         *ent*nehmen   to take from, to deduce

         laufen   to run
         *ent*laufen   to run away, to escape

         ziehen   to pull, to move
         *ent*ziehen   to move away from, to remove

er-   usually makes a verb transitive; frequently implies acquisition of some
         object by means of the verb
         kämpfen   to fight
         *er*kämpfen   to win something in a fight

         richten   to put something right
         *er*richten   to set up, to build, to erect

         zwingen   to force
         *er*zwingen   to get by force

ver-   reverses the verb action; frequently implies deviation from the verb action
         kaufen   to buy
         *ver*kaufen   to sell

         mieten   to rent from someone
         *ver*mieten   to lease to someone

         passen   to suit, to be suitable
         *ver*passen   to miss out on something

         sagen   to say
         *ver*sagen   to fail at something

zer-   an extreme verb action, implies "completely" or "to pieces"
         stören   to disturb
         *zer*stören   to destroy

         fallen   to fall
         *zer*fallen   to fall to pieces, to decay

         brechen   to break
         *zer*brechen   to shatter

Separable and Inseparable Prefixes

A number of prefixes can be either separable or inseparable, although, when they are used with the same verb, the meaning of the verb is different in each case. The most common of these prefixes are *durch-, um-,* and *unter-*. Note that, when a prefix is separable, it is stressed in speech. When the prefix is inseparable, the verb (stem) is stressed.

*dúrch*reisen	(separable)	to travel through
*durch*réisen	(inseparable)	to traverse
*durch*súchen	(inseparable)	to search through, to frisk
*úm*schreiben	(separable)	to rewrite
*um*schréiben	(inseparable)	to paraphrase
*unter*bréchen	(inseparable)	to interrupt
*únter*gehen	(separable)	to go under, to decline
*unter*súchen	(inseparable)	to investigate

13. The Imperative

1. The imperative is used to issue commands and requests. In English, examples include:

Open the door!	Let's go to the movies!
Stand up!	Let's stay home this evening!
Turn off the television!	Let's see the parade!

2. Since German has three forms corresponding to "you," there are three corresponding forms of the imperative. The *Sie*-imperative involves taking the present tense *Sie*-form of the verb and placing the *Sie* after the verb:

Stehen Sie auf!	Stand/Get up!
Kommen Sie her!	Come here!
Trinken Sie den Kaffee!	Drink the coffee!
Fahren Sie geradeaus!	Drive straight ahead!

3. The *ihr*-imperative is simpler yet. It is merely the present tense *ihr*-form of the verb in question without the *ihr*.

Steht auf!	Stand up!
Kommt her!	Come here!
Trinkt nicht so viel Kaffee!	Don't drink so much coffee!
Fahrt immer geradeaus weiter!	Keep on driving straight ahead!

4. The *du*-imperative is created by taking the *du*-form of the present tense and removing the *-st* ending.

Steh auf!	Stand up!
Komm her!	Come here!
Gib mir die Zeitung!	Give me the newspaper!
Schrei nicht so laut!	Don't yell so loud!
Mach die Tür endlich zu!	Close the door once and for all!

Exception: Verbs that change their stem from *a* to *ä* in the present tense do *not* make this change in the *du*-imperative.

Fahr weiter!	Drive on!
Trag diese Tasche!	Carry this bag!
Fall nicht vom Stuhl!	Don't fall off the chair!

5. The form of the imperative corresponding to English "Let's... is formed by taking the *wir*-form of the present tense and putting the pronoun *wir* after it:

Gehen wir jetzt nach Hause!	Let's go home now!
Schreiben wir an die Großmutter!	Let's write Grandmother!
Trinken wir ein Bier!	Let's drink a beer!

6. The imperative forms of *sein* are:

Seien Sie so lieb!	Be kind!
Seid freundlich!	Be friendly!
Sei gut!	Be good!
Seien wir ehrlich miteinander!	Let's be honest with each other!

7. There is a form of imperative that is used in street signs, warnings, recipes, and abrupt verbal exchanges. It involves an abbreviated sentence that omits the subject (*Sie, du, ihr*) and the modal verb (*nicht dürfen, müssen, sollen, nicht sollen*).

(Sie müssen) aufpassen.	(You have to) watch out.
Aufpassen!	Watch out!
Bitte nicht stören!	Please do not disturb!
Einfahrt freihalten!	Do not block the entrance!
Nicht ohne Batterie fahren!	Do not operate vehicle without the battery!
Vor Weihnachten nicht aufmachen!	Do not open before Christmas!
Eine Stunde bei 200 Grad backen!	Bake one hour at 200 degrees!

14. Present Tense of the Subjunctive

There are two sets of subjunctive tenses in German, the *hypothetical* and the *indirect discourse.*

The subjunctive mood is used to put distance between the speaker or writer and what he/she says or writes. It expresses wishes, statements contrary to fact, politeness, and indirectness. Examples of the subjunctive in English include:

I would like to go home now.
We would fly to the Bahamas, if we had the money!
They should have left yesterday.
If they had only left when we told them to!
He said he was going to come over later.

Hypothetical Subjunctive

1. The hypothetical subjunctive is by far the more common of the two sets of subjunctive tenses, and frequently serves the functions of both. The present tense hypothetical subjunctive is formed off the preterite stem of the indicative.*
To this stem are added the following endings, if they are not already present.

ich	-e		*wir*	-en
du	-est		*ihr*	-et
man	-e		*sie*	-en

*Note: The term *indicative* refers to all the tense forms met up to now, with the exception of *imperative*. The terms *indicative, imperative,* and *subjunctive* are the three moods of German and English verbs.

2. In the case of most weak verbs the forms thus generated are exactly the same as the preterite indicative:

> *machen* to do, to make
> (if) I did, (if) you did, etc.

ich machte	wir machten
du machtest	ihr machtet
man machte	sie machten

3. In the case of most strong verbs, the forms take an umlaut in their stem as well as the above endings:

sein to be

(if) I were, (if) you were, etc.

ich wäre	wir wären
du wärest	ihr wäret
man wäre	sie wären

Wenn ich ein Vöglein wär(e),	If I were a little bird,
Und auch zwei Flüglein hätt(e),	And had two little wings,
Flög(e) ich zu dir.	I would fly to you.
(Deutsches Volkslied)	(German folksong)

4. In practice, only a handful of verbs use their "pure" present subjunctive, in modern German. These include:

Infinitive	Present Subjunctive	
dürfen	**dürfte**	I might be permitted to
geben	**gäbe**	I would give
gehen	**ginge**	I would go
haben	**hätte**	I would have
kommen	**käme**	I would come
können	**könnte**	I might be able to, I could
lassen	**liesse**	I might permit, I might have (something) done
mögen	**möchte**	I would like to
sein	**wäre**	I would be
sollen*	**sollte**	I should, I ought to
werden	**würde**	I would
wissen	**wüßte**	I would know
wollen*	**wollte**	I would want to

*Note: *Sollen* and *wollen* do not take an umlaut in the subjunctive.

5. Most verbs use the appropriate present subjunctive of *werden* plus the infinitive just like the modal verb.

machen to do, to make

I would do, you would do, etc.

ich würde...machen	**wir würden...machen**
du würdest...machen	**ihr würdet...machen**
man würde...machen	**sie würden...machen**

As in the future tense with *werden*, the infinitive after *würde* will stand at the end of the sentence.

Wenn ich viel Geld hätte, würde ich ein großes Haus kaufen.	If I had a lot of money, I would buy a big house.
Wenn wir alle reich wären, würden wir auch unglücklich sein.	If we all were rich, we would also be unhappy.
Wenn ich besser schreiben könnte, würde ich viel schreiben.	If I could write better, I would write more.

6. This form of the subjunctive is also called the *general subjunctive, conditional, subjunctive II,* and even the *past subjunctive* (both present and past tense forms). The *würde*-subjunctive is also sometimes referred to as the *future subjunctive,* even though the hypothetical subjunctive cannot have either a present or a future, only a past and a "nonpast."

Indirect Discourse Subjunctive

1. The second form of the subjunctive is used almost exclusively to report statements made in writing or in spoken language by people other than the writer or speaker. English has a similar construction, using what looks like the past tense to render what someone said in the present.

> He said, "I am going home."
> He said that he *was going* home.

> She quoted him as saying, "I will not work here any more!"
> She quoted him as saying that he *would not work* here any more.

> I overheard them say, "We took the money and ran."
> I overheard them say that they *had taken* the money and *run.*

2. The indirect discourse subjunctive is sometimes also called *subjunctive I, special subjunctive,* and even the *present subjunctive.* Its forms represent the most regular tense in the German language, although its use is highly restricted. It uses the same endings as the hypothetical subjunctive.

ich	*-e*		**wir**	*-en*
du	*-est*		**ihr**	*-et*
man	*-e*		**sie**	*-en*

machen   to do, to make
(He said that...) I do, you do, etc.

ich mache	**wir machen**
du machest	**ihr machet**
man mache	**sie machen**

However, the indirect discourse subjunctive does not use the preterite as a base. Instead, it uses the present tense stem without any changes (that is, stem-vowel changes such as those found in *geben, lesen, fahren, stossen* etc., do not apply).

sehen   to see
(She said that...) I see, you see, etc.

ich sehe	**wir sehen**
du sehest	**ihr sehet**
man sehe	**sie sehen**

geben   to give
(You said that...) I give, you give, etc.

ich gebe	wir geben
du gebest	ihr gebet
man gebe	sie geben

tragen   to wear, to carry
(I said that...) I wear, you wear, etc.

ich trage	wir tragen
du tragest	ihr traget
man trage	sie tragen

Der Präsident sagte, daß er eine verbesserte Zukunft sehe. Es gebe immer noch 12% Arbeitlosigkeit. Das Volk trage aber diese Last mit Geduld. (an example of extended indirect discourse)	The president said that he saw an improved future. There was still 12% unemployment. The people were, however, bearing this burden with patience.

3. The forms of the indirect discourse subjunctive are so regular that only *sein* has any irregularities, namely, no -e in the *ich* and *man* forms.

sein   to be
(They said that...) I am, you are, etc.

ich sei	wir seien
du seiest	ihr seiet
man sei	sie seien

Der Minister sagte, daß er mit dem Vertrag einverstanden sei. Die Bedingungen seien alle in Ordnung. Die beiden Länder seien ausgezeichnete Handelspartner. (an example of extended indirect discourse)	The minister said that he was satisfied with the treaty. The terms were all in order. The two countries were excellent trading partners.

The Future Tense of the Indirect Discourse Subjunctive

The indirect discourse subjunctive can have a future tense, unlike the hypothetical subjunctive. This is formed exactly like the future indicative or the subjunctive with *würde*, except that the indirect discourse subjunctive of *werden* is used:

machen   to do, to make
(She said that...) I will do, you will do, etc.

ich werde...machen	wir werden...machen
du werdest...machen	ihr werdet...machen
man werde...machen	sie werden...machen

Der Minister sagte, daß er den Vertrag unterschreiben werde.	He said that he would sign the treaty.
Er meinte, daß der Vertrag die Zusammenarbeit erleichtern werde.	He was of the opinion that the treaty would make cooperation much easier.

15. Past Tense of the Subjunctive

The subjunctive can have a past tense, since there are situations where what might have occured did not in fact occur.

If we hadn't taken the car, we would have been late.
She would have been hurt, if she hadn't been an expert skier.

The subjunctive has only one past tense form, resembling the present perfect of the indicative. There is no preterite subjunctive. The past tense of the hypothetical subjunctive is created by using the appropriate form of *haben* or *sein* in the subjunctive plus the past participle.

machen   to do, to make
I would have done, you would have done, etc.

ich hätte (habe)...gemacht	wir hätten (haben)...gemacht
du hättest (habest)...gemacht	ihr hättet (habet)...gemacht
man hätte (habe)...gemacht	sie hätten (haben)...gemacht

gehen   to go
I would have gone, you would have gone, etc.

ich wäre (sei)...gegangen	wir wären (seien)...gegangen
du wärest (seiest)...gegangen	ihr wäret (seiest)...gegangen
man wäre (sei)...gegangen	sie wären (seien)...gegangen

Ich hätte das gemacht, wenn ich Zeit gehabt hätte.	I would have done that, if I had had time.
Wären wir doch alle zusammen ins Kino gegangen!	If only we had all gone together to the movies!
Er behauptet, er habe nichts gesehen.	He claims (that) he saw nothing.

Note: All modals take *haben* in the present perfect, whether indicative or subjunctive. The infinitive of the main verb is not relevant.

Wir hätten das nicht machen sollen.	We should not have done that.
Er hätte mitgehen können, wenn er das gewußt hätte.	He could have gone along, if he had known about it.

16. The Passive Voice

1. The passive voice is used to emphasize the activity performed, not the person performing the activity. In English, the passive is formed by using the appropriate form of "to be" plus the past participle.

Bananas are grown in many tropical countries.
Elk have been spotted again in those mountains.
Letters are more easily typed than handwritten.

2. In German, the passive voice is created by using *werden* plus the past participle placed at the end of the clause.

sehen   to see
I am seen, you are seen, etc.

ich werde...gesehen	**wir werden...gesehen**
du wirst...gesehen	**ihr werdet...gesehen**
man wird...gesehen	**sie werden...gesehen**

Ich sehe und (ich) *werde gesehen*.	I see and am seen.
Ich höre und (ich) *werde gehört*.	I hear and am heard.
Ich rufe und (ich) *werde gerufen*.	I call and am called.
Bücher *werden* überall in der Bundesrepublik *gelesen*.	Books are read everywhere in the Federal Republic.
Ein Freund *wird* immer gern *eingeladen*.	A friend is always invited gladly.

3. The preterite passive uses the preterite of *werden.*

sehen   to see
I was seen, you were seen, etc.

ich wurde...gesehen	**wir wurden...gesehen**
du wurdest...gesehen	**ihr wurdet...gesehen**
man wurde...gesehen	**sie wurden...gesehen**

Ich sah and *wurde gesehen*.	I saw and was seen.
Ich hörte und *wurde gehört*.	I heard and was heard.
Bücher *wurden* schon im siebzehnten Jahrhundert in Deutschland *gedruckt*.	Books were already being printed in Germany in the seventeenth century.
Mein Freund Hans *wurde* von uns gestern *eingeladen*.	My friend Hans was invited by us yesterday.

4. The perfect passive tenses have patterns similar to their corresponding active (nonpassive) ones. But instead of *geworden* for the past participle of *werden,* an abbreviated form is used: *worden.* Remember that *werden* (*wurde, geworden/ worden*) requires the appropriate forms of *sein* in its compound tenses.

sehen   to see

I have been seen, you have been seen, etc.

ich bin...gesehen worden	**wir sind...gesehen worden**
du bist...gesehen worden	**ihr seid...gesehen worden**
man ist...gesehen worden	**sie sind...gesehen worden**

Ich habe gesehen und *bin gesehen worden.*	I have seen and have been seen.
Bücher *sind* **schon im 17. Jahrhundert in Deutschland** *gedruckt worden.*	Books were printed in the 17th century in Germany.
Mein Freund *ist* **von uns** *eingeladen worden.*	My friend was/has been invited by us.

5. The future passive simply requires the future forms of *werden.*

sehen   to see

I will be seen, you will be seen, etc.

ich werde...gesehen werden	**wir werden...gesehen werden**
du wirst...gesehen werden	**ihr werdet...gesehen werden**
man wird...gesehen werden	**sie werden...gesehen werden**

Ich werde sehen und *werde gesehen werden.*	I will see and will be seen.
Bücher *werden* **hoffentlich auch im 21. Jahrhundert** *gedruckt werden.*	Books will hopefully be printed in the 21st century, too.

6. Other passive tenses follow patterns similar to those for the active tenses.

Past Perfect:

Ich hatte gesehen und *war gesehen worden.*	I had seen and had been seen.

Future Perfect:

Ich werde gesehen haben und *werde gesehen worden sein.*	I will have seen and will have been seen.

Present Subjunctive:

Ich würde sehen und *würde gesehen werden.*	I would see and would be seen.

Past Subjunctive:

Ich hätte gesehen und *wäre gesehen worden.*	I would have seen and would have been seen.

7. When the agent (doer) must be expressed in German, the preposition *von* (''by'') is used.

Ich sehe ihn.	I see him.
Er wird *von mir* gesehen.	He is seen *by me.*
Er sieht mich.	He sees me.
Ich werde *von ihm* gesehen.	I am seen *by him.*

17. Summary of Verb Forms

Major Patterns

All inflected verbs, that is, verbs with endings, have at least the following endings, depending on the person and number of the subject of the verb to which they are attached.

ich	-		*wir*	**-n**
du	**-st**		*ihr*	**-t**
man	—		*sie*	**-n**

The following verbs represent all major inflectional patterns of German verbs: *empfehlen, haben, kommen, können, sein, suchen, werden.*

Although all the forms of *haben, sein,* and *werden* have already been presented, they are brought together here for easier reference. *Machen* has been used to illustrate the basic patterns of weak verbs; *suchen* will be used to give the reader another verb to look at. *Können* represents the modals. *Empfehlen* represents verbs with a stem-vowel change in the present tense as well as a verb with an inseparable prefix. *Kommen* represents verbs conjugated with *sein* in the perfect tenses.

The order of presentation of the tenses follows that used in this book.

empfehlen   to recommend

Present: *I recommend, etc.*

ich empfehle	**wir empfehlen**
du empfiehlst	**ihr empfehlt**
man empfiehlt	**sie empfehlen**

Future: *I will recommend, etc.*

ich werde...empfehlen	**wir werden...empfehlen**
du wirst...empfehlen	**ihr werdet...empfehlen**
man wird...empfehlen	**sie werden...empfehlen**

Preterite: *I recommended, etc.*

ich empfahl	**wir empfahlen**
du empfahlst	**ihr empfahlt**
man empfahl	**sie empfahlen**

Present Perfect: *I recommended, I have recommended, etc.*

ich habe...empfohlen	**wir haben...empfohlen**
du hast...empfohlen	**ihr habt...empfohlen**
man hat...empfohlen	**sie haben...empfohlen**

Past Perfect: *I had recommended, etc.*

ich hatte...empfohlen	wir hatten...empfohlen
du hattest...empfohlen	ihr hattet...empfohlen
man hatte...empfohlen	sie hatten...empfohlen

Future perfect: *I will have recommended, etc.*

ich werde...empfohlen haben	wir werden...empfohlen haben
du wirst...empfohlen haben	ihr werdet...empfohlen haben
man wird...empfohlen haben	sie werden...empfohlen haben

Imperative: *Recommend! Let's recommend!*

(du) **empfiehl!** recommend!
(wir) **empfehlen wir!** let's recommend!
(ihr) **empfehlt!**
(Sie) **empfehlen Sie!**

Present Subjunctive without *würde: I would recommend, etc.*

ich empfähle	wir empfählen
du empfählest	ihr empfählet
man empfähle	sie empfählen

Present Subjunctive with *würde: I would recommend, etc.*

ich würde...empfehlen	wir würden...empfehlen
du würdest...empfehlen	ihr würdet...empfehlen
man würde...empfehlen	sie würden...empfehlen

Present Subjunctive (indirect discourse): *(He said that...) I recommend, etc.*

ich empfehle	wir empfehlen
du empfehlest	ihr empfehlet
man empfehle	sie empfehlen

Future Subjunctive (indirect discourse): *(They said that...) I will recommend, etc.*

ich werde...empfehlen	wir werden...empfehlen
du werdest...empfehlen	ihr werdet...empfehlen
man werde...empfehlen	sie werden...empfehlen

Past Subjunctive *I would have recommended, etc.*

ich hätte...empfohlen	wir hätten...empfohlen
du hättest...empfohlen	ihr hättet...empfohlen
man hätte...empfohlen	sie hätten...empfohlen

Past Subjunctive (indirect discourse): *(She said that...) I had recommended, etc.*

ich habe...empfohlen	wir haben...empfohlen
du habest...empfohlen	ihr habet...empfohlen
man habe...empfohlen	sie haben...empfohlen

Present Passive: *I am (being) recommended, etc.*

ich werde...empfohlen	wir werden...empfohlen
du wirst...empfohlen	ihr werdet...empfohlen
man wird...empfohlen	sie werden...empfohlen

Preterite Passive: *I was (being) recommended, etc.*

ich wurde...empfohlen	wir wurden...empfohlen
du wurdest...empfohlen	ihr wurdet...empfohlen
man wurde...empfohlen	sie wurden...empfohlen

Present Perfect Passive: *I was (being) recommended, I have been recommended, etc.*

ich bin...empfohlen worden	wir sind...empfohlen worden
du bist...empfohlen worden	ihr seid...empfohlen worden
man ist...empfohlen worden	sie sind...empfohlen worden

Past Perfect Passive: *I had been recommended, etc.*

ich war...empfohlen worden	wir waren...empfohlen worden
du warst...empfohlen worden	ihr wart...empfohlen worden
man war...empfohlen worden	sie waren...empfohlen worden

Future Passive: *I will be recommended, etc.*

ich werde...empfohlen werden	wir werden...empfohlen werden
du wirst...empfohlen werden	ihr werdet...empfohlen werden
man wird...empfohlen werden	sie werden...empfohlen werden

haben   to have

Present: *I have, etc.*

ich habe	wir haben
du hast	ihr habt
man hat	sie haben

Future: *I will have, etc.*

ich werde...haben	wir werden...haben
du wirst...haben	ihr werdet...haben
man wird...haben	sie werden...haben

Preterite: *I had, etc.*

ich hatte	wir hatten
du hattest	ihr hattet
man hatte	sie hatten

Present Perfect: *I had, I have had, etc.*

ich habe...gehabt	wir haben...gehabt
du hast...gehabt	ihr habt...gehabt
man hat...gehabt	sie haben...gehabt

Past Perfect: *I had had, etc.*

ich hatte...gehabt	wir hatten...gehabt
du hattest...gehabt	ihr hattet...gehabt
man hatte...gehabt	sie hatten...gehabt

Future Perfect: *I will have had, etc.*

ich werde...gehabt haben	wir werden...gehabt haben
du wirst...gehabt haben	ihr werdet...gehabt haben
man wird...gehabt haben	sie werden...gehabt haben

Imperative: *Have! Let's have!*

(du)	hab(e)!
(wir)	haben wir!
(ihr)	habt!
(Sie)	haben Sie!

Present Subjunctive without *würde: I would have, etc.*

ich hätte	wir hätten
du hättest	ihr hättet
man hätte	sie hätten

Present Subjunctive with *würde**

*Note: These forms are normally not used. Hereafter, forms that are not used will not be listed.

Present Subjunctive (indirect discourse): *(I said that...) I have, etc.*

ich habe	wir haben
du habest	ihr habet
man habe	sie haben

Future Subjunctive (indirect discourse): *(You said that...) I will have, etc.*

ich werde...haben	wir werden...haben
du werdest...haben	ihr werdet...haben
man werde...haben	sie werden...haben

Past Subjunctive: *I would have had, etc.*

ich hätte...gehabt	wir hätten...gehabt
du hättest...gehabt	ihr hättet...gehabt
man hätte...gehabt	sie hätten...gehabt

Past Subjunctive (indirect discourse): *(We said that...) I had, etc.*

ich habe...gehabt	wir haben...gehabt
du habest...gehabt	ihr habet...gehabt
man habe...gehabt	sie haben...gehabt

Present Passive**

ich werde...gehabt	wir werden...gehabt
du wirst...gehabt	ihr werdet...gehabt
man wird...gehabt	sie werden...gehabt

Preterite Passive**

ich wurde...gehabt	wir wurden...gehabt
du wurdest...gehabt	ihr wurdet...gehabt
man wurde...gehabt	sie wurden...gehabt

Present Perfect Passive**

ich bin...gehabt worden	wir sind...gehabt worden
du bist...gehabt worden	ihr seid...gehabt worden
man ist...gehabt worden	sie sind...gehabt worden

Past Perfect Passive**

ich war...gehabt worden	wir waren...gehabt worden
du warst...gehabt worden	ihr wart...gehabt worden
man war...gehabt worden	sie waren...gehabt worden

Future Passive**

ich werde...gehabt werden	wir werden...gehabt werden
du wirst...gehabt werden	ihr werdet...gehabt werden
man wird...gehabt werden	sie werden...gehabt werden

**Note: *Haben* is rarely used in the passive voice, although there are verbs with prefixes that do have passive forms, such as *vorhaben* (separable) "to intend," "to plan;" *handhaben* "to operate," "to manipulate." The passive forms of *haben* are listed here for reference only. English "have" in the sense of "I had cereal for breakfast" or "We have been had by the government" cannot normally be translated as *haben* in German.

kommen   to come

Present: *I come, I am coming, etc.*

ich komme	wir kommen
du kommst	ihr kommt
man kommt	sie kommen

Future: *I will come, etc.*

ich werde...kommen	wir werden...kommen
du wirst...kommen	ihr werdet...kommen
man wird...kommen	sie werden...kommen

Preterite: *I came, etc.*

ich kam	wir kamen
du kamst	ihr kamt
man kam	sie kamen

Present Perfect: *I came, I have come, etc.*

ich bin...gekommen	wir sind...gekommen
du bist...gekommen	ihr seid...gekommen
man ist...gekommen	sie sind...gekommen

Past Perfect: *I had come, etc.*

ich war...gekommen	wir waren...gekommen
du warst...gekommen	ihr wart...gekommen
man war...gekommen	sie waren...gekommen

Future Perfect: *I will have come, etc.*

ich werde...gekommen sein	wir werden...gekommen sein
du wirst...gekommen sein	ihr werdet...gekommen sein
man wird...gekommen sein	sie werden...gekommen sein

Imperative: *Come! Let's come!*

(du)	komm!
(wir)	kommen wir!
(ihr)	kommt!
(Sie)	kommen Sie!

Present Subjunctive without *würde: I would come, etc.*

ich käme	wir kämen
du kämest	ihr kämet
man käme	sie kämen

Present Subjunctive with *würde: I would come, etc.*

ich würde...kommen	wir würden...kommen
du würdest...kommen	ihr würdet...kommen
man würde...kommen	sie würden...kommen

Present Subjunctive (indirect discourse): *(I said that... I come, etc.)*

ich komme	wir kommen
du kommest	ihr kommet
man komme	sie kommen

Future Subjunctive (indirect discourse): *(She said that...) I will come, etc.*

ich werde...kommen	wir werden...kommen
du werdest...kommen	ihr werdet...kommen
man werde...kommen	sie werden...kommen

Past Subjunctive: *I would have come, etc.*

ich wäre...gekommen	wir wären...gekommen
du wärest...gekommen	ihr wäret...gekommen
man wäre...gekommen	sie wären...gekommen

Past Subjunctive (indirect discourse): *(They said that...) I have come, etc.*

ich sei...gekommen	wir seien...gekommen
du seiest...gekommen	ihr seiet...gekommen
man sei...gekommen	sie seien...gekommen

können   to be able to
Present: *I can, I am able to, etc.*

ich kann
du kannst
man kann

wir können
ihr könnt
sie können

Future: *I will be able to, etc.*

ich werde...können
du wirst...können
man wird...können

wir werden...können
ihr werdet...können
sie werden...können

Preterite: *I was able to, I could, etc.*

ich konnte
du konntest
man konnte

wir konnten
ihr konntet
sie konnten

Present Perfect: *I was able to, I have been able to, etc.*

ich habe...können (gekonnt)
du hast...können (gekonnt)
man hat...können (gekonnt)

wir haben...können (gekonnt)
ihr habt...können (gekonnt)
sie haben...können (gekonnt)

Past Perfect: *I had been able to, etc.*

ich hatte ...können (gekonnt)
du hattest...können (gekonnt)
man hatte...können (gekonnt)

wir hatten...können (gekonnt)
ihr hattet...können (gekonnt)
sie hatten...können (gekonnt)

Present Subjunctive without *würde: I would be able to, I could, etc.*

ich könnte
du könntest
man könnte

wir könnten
ihr könntet
sie könnten

Present Subjunctive (indirect discourse): *(I said that...) I would be able to, etc.*

ich könne
du könnest
man könne

wir können
ihr könnet
sie können

Future Subjunctive (indirect discourse): *(He said that...) I will be able to, etc.*

ich werde...können
du werdest...können
man werde...können

wir werden...können
ihr werdet...können
sie werden...können

Past Subjunctive: *I would have been able to, etc.*

ich hätte...können (gekonnt)
du hättest...können (gekonnt)
man hätte...können (gekonnt)

wir hätten...können (gekonnt)
ihr hättet...können (gekonnt)
sie hätten...können (gekonnt)

Past Subjunctive (indirect discourse:) *(We said that...) I was able to, etc.*

ich habe...können (gekonnt)	wir haben...können (gekonnt)
du habest...können (gekonnt)	ihr habet...können (gekonnt)
man habe...können (gekonnt)	sie haben...können (gekonnt)

sein   to be

Present: *I am, etc.*

ich bin	wir sind
du bist	ihr seid
man ist	sie sind

Future: *I will be, etc.*

ich werde...sein	wir werden...sein
du wirst...sein	ihr werdet...sein
man wird...sein	sie werden...sein

Preterite: *I was, etc.*

ich war	wir waren
du warst	ihr wart
man war	sie waren

Present Perfect: *I was, I have been, etc.*

ich bin...gewesen	wir sind...gewesen
du bist...gewesen	ihr seid...gewesen
man ist...gewesen	sie sind...gewesen

Past Perfect: *I had been, etc.*

ich war...gewesen	wir waren...gewesen
du warst...gewesen	ihr wart...gewesen
man war...gewesen	sie waren...gewesen

Future Perfect: *I will have been, etc.*

ich werde...gewesen sein	wir werden...gewesen sein
du wirst...gewesen sein	ihr werdet...gewesen sein
man wird...gewesen sein	sie werden...gewesen sein

Imperative: *Be!, Let's be!*

(du)	sei!
(wir)	seien wir!
(ihr)	seid!
(Sie)	seien Sie!

Present Subjunctive without *würde: I would be, etc.*

ich wäre	wir wären
du wärest	ihr wäret
man wäre	sie wären

Present Subjunctive (indirect discourse): *(She said that...) I am, etc.*

ich sei	wir seien
du seiest	ihr seiet
man sei	sie seien

Future Subjunctive (indirect discourse): *(They said that...) I will be, etc.*

ich werde...sein	wir werden...sein
du werdest...sein	ihr werdet...sein
man werde...sein	sie werden...sein

Past Subjunctive: *I would have been, etc.*

ich wäre...gewesen	wir wären...gewesen
du wärest...gewesen	ihr wäret...gewesen
man wäre...gewesen	sie wären...gewesen

Past Subjunctive (indirect discourse): *(He said that...) I was, etc.*

ich sei...gewesen	wir seien...gewesen
du seiest...gewesen	ihr seiet...gewesen
man sei...gewesen	sie seien...gewesen

suchen　to look for

Present: *I look for, etc.*

ich suche	wir suchen
du suchst	ihr sucht
man sucht	sie suchen

Future: *I will look for, etc.*

ich werde...suchen	wir werden...suchen
du wirst...suchen	ihr werdet...suchen
man wird...suchen	sie werden...suchen

Preterite: *I looked for, etc.*

ich suchte	wir suchten
du suchtest	ihr suchtet
man suchte	sie suchten

Present Perfect: *I looked for, I have looked for, etc.*

ich habe...gesucht	wir haben...gesucht
du hast...gesucht	ihr habt...gesucht
man hat...gesucht	sie haben...gesucht

Past Perfect: *I had looked for, etc.*

ich hatte...gesucht	wir hatten...gesucht
du hattest...gesucht	ihr hattet...gesucht
man hatte...gesucht	sie hatten...gesucht

Future Perfect: *I will have looked for, etc.*

ich werde...gesucht haben   wir werden...gesucht haben
du wirst...gesucht haben   ihr werdet...gesucht haben
man wird...gesucht haben   sie werden...gesucht haben

Imperative: *Look for!, Let's look for!*

(du)   such(e)!
(wir) suchen wir!
(ihr) sucht!
(Sie) suchen Sie!

Present Subjunctive without *würde: I would look for, etc.*

ich suchte   wir suchten
du suchtest   ihr suchtet
man suchte   sie suchten

Present Subjunctive with *würde: I would look for, etc.*

ich würde...suchen   wir würden...suchen
du würdest...suchen   ihr würdet...suchen
man würde...suchen   sie würden...suchen

Present Subjunctive (indirect discourse): *(You said that...) I look for, etc.*

ich suche   wir suchen
du suchest   ihr suchet
man suche   sie suchen

Future Subjunctive (indirect discourse): *(We said that...) I will look for, etc.*

ich werde...suchen   wir werden...suchen
du werdest...suchen   ihr werdet...suchen
man werde...suchen   sie werden...suchen

Past Subjunctive: *I would have looked for, etc.*

ich hätte...gesucht   wir hätten...gesucht
du hättest...gesucht   ihr hättet...gesucht
man hätte...gesucht   sie hätten...gesucht

Past Subjunctive (indirect discourse): *(They said that...) I looked for, etc.*

ich habe...gesucht   wir haben...gesucht
du habest...gesucht   ihr habet...gesucht
man habe...gesucht   sie haben...gesucht

Present Passive: *I am (being) looked for, etc.*

ich werde...gesucht   wir werden...gesucht
du wirst...gesucht   ihr werdet...gesucht
man wird...gesucht   sie werden...gesucht

Preterite Passive: *I was (being) looked for, etc.*

ich wurde...gesucht	wir wurden...gesucht
du wurdest...gesucht	ihr wurdet...gesucht
man wurde...gesucht	sie wurden...gesucht

Present Perfect Passive: *I was (being) looked for, I have been looked for, etc.*

ich bin...gesucht worden	wir sind...gesucht worden
du bist...gesucht worden	ihr seid...gesucht worden
man ist...gesucht worden	sie sind...gesucht worden

Past Perfect Passive: *I had been looked for, etc.*

ich war...gesucht worden	wir waren...gesucht worden
du warst...gesucht worden	ihr wart...gesucht worden
man war...gesucht worden	sie waren...gesucht worden

Future Passive: *I will have been looked for, etc.*

ich werde...gesucht werden	wir werden...gesucht werden
du wirst...gesucht werden	ihr werdet...gesucht werden
man wird...gesucht werden	sie werden...gesucht werden

werden   to become

Present: *I become, etc.*

ich werde	wir werden
du wirst	ihr werdet
man wird	sie werden

Future: *I will become, etc.*

ich werde...werden	wir werden...werden
du wirst...werden	ihr werdet...werden
man wird...werden	sie werden...werden

Preterite: *I became, etc.*

ich würde	wir würden
du würdest	ihr würdet
man würde	sie würden

Present Perfect: *I became, I have become, etc.*

ich bin...geworden	wir sind...geworden
du bist...geworden	ihr seid...geworden
man ist...geworden	sie sind...geworden

Past Perfect: *I had become, etc.*

ich war...geworden	wir waren...geworden
du warst...geworden	ihr wart...geworden
man war...geworden	sie waren...geworden

Future Perfect: *I will have become, etc.*

ich werde...geworden sein	wir werden...geworden sein
du wirst...geworden sein	ihr werdet...geworden sein
man wird...geworden sein	sie werden...geworden sein

Present Subjunctive without *würde: I would become, etc.*

ich würde	wir würden
du würdest	ihr würdet
man würde	sie würden

Present Subjunctive with *würde: I would become, etc.*

ich würde...werden	wir würden...werden
du würdest...werden	ihr würdet...werden
man würde...werden	sie würden...werden

Present Subjunctive (indirect discourse): *(He said that...) I become, etc.*

ich werde	wir werden
du werdest	ihr werdet
man werde	sie werden

Future Subjunctive (indirect discourse): *(We said that...) I will become, etc.*

ich werde...werden	wir werden...werden
du werdest...werden	ihr werdet...werden
man werde...werden	sie werden...werden

Past Subjunctive: *I would have become, etc.*

ich wäre...geworden	wir wären...geworden
du wärest...geworden	ihr wäret...geworden
man wäre...geworden	sie wären...geworden

Past Subjunctive (indirect discourse): *(I said that...) I became, etc.*

ich sei...geworden	wir seien...geworden
du seiest...geworden	ihr seiet...geworden
man sei...geworden	sie seien...geworden

Principal Parts

Strong Verbs

The following is a list of the most common strong verbs and their principal parts. (*S* indicates a verb that takes *sein* in its compound tenses. * indicates a verb with a prefix that takes *haben*, even though its base verb takes *sein*. For example, *Er ist gefahren*, but *Er hat erfahren*.)

Infinitive	Preterite	Past Participle	
beginnen	**begann**	**begonnen**	to begin
bieten	**bot**	**geboten**	to offer
anbieten	**bot...an**	**angeboten**	to make an offer
verbieten	**verbot**	**verboten**	to forbid
binden	**band**	**gebunden**	to tie, to bind
bitten	**bat**	**gebeten**	to ask (a favor)
bleiben	**blieb**	**geblieben (S)**	to stay, to remain
brechen (bricht)	**brach**	**gebrochen**	to break
zerbrechen (zerbricht)	**zerbrach**	**zerbrochen**	to shatter
bringen	**brachte**	**gebracht**	to bring
verbringen	**verbrachte**	**verbracht**	to spend (time)
denken	**dachte**	**gedacht**	to think
dürfen (darf)	**durfte**	**dürfen (gedurft)**	to be allowed to
empfehlen (empfiehlt)	**empfahl**	**empfohlen**	to recommend
essen (ißt)	**aß**	**gegessen**	to eat
fahren (fährt)	**fuhr**	**gefahren (S)**	to go by vehicle
erfahren (erfährt)	**erfuhr**	**erfahren***	to learn about something
fallen (fällt)	**fiel**	**gefallen (S)**	to fall
gefallen (gefällt)	**gefiel**	**gefallen***	to please
fangen (fängt)	**fing**	**gefangen**	to catch
anfangen (fängt ...an)	**fing ...an**	**angefangen**	to begin
finden	**fand**	**gefunden**	to find
erfinden	**erfand**	**erfunden**	to invent
geben (gibt)	**gab**	**gegeben**	to give
aufgeben (gibt ...auf)	**gab ...auf**	**aufgegeben**	to give up
ausgeben (gibt ...aus)	**gab ...aus**	**ausgegeben**	to spend (money)
umgeben (umgibt)	**umgab**	**umgeben**	to surround
gehen	**ging**	**gegangen (S)**	to go
begehen	**beging**	**begangen***	to commit (a crime)
geniessen	**genoß**	**genossen**	to enjoy
greifen	**griff**	**gegriffen**	to grasp
begreifen	**begriff**	**begriffen**	to comprehend
haben (hat)	**hatte**	**gehabt**	to have
vorhaben (hat...vor)	**hatte...vor**	**vorgehabt**	to intend
halten (hält)	**hielt**	**gehalten**	to hold, to stop
behalten (behält)	**behielt**	**behalten**	to keep
erhalten (erhält)	**erhielt**	**erhalten**	to receive
hängen	**hing**	**gehangen**	to hang
heben	**hob**	**gehoben**	to lift
heißen	**hieß**	**geheissen**	to be named
helfen (hilft)	**half**	**geholfen**	to help

Infinitive	Preterite	Past Participle	
kennen	kannte	gekannt	to know (a person)
erkennen	erkannte	erkannt	to recognize
kommen	kam	gekommen (*S*)	to come
bekommen	bekam	bekommen*	to get, to obtain
können (kann)	konnte	können (gekonnt)	to be able to
laden (lädt)	lud	geladen	to load
einladen (lädt ...ein)	lud ...ein	eingeladen	to invite
lassen (lässt)	ließ	gelassen	to have (something done)
verlassen (verlässt)	verließ	verlassen	to abandon
laufen (läuft)	lief	gelaufen (*S*)	to run
leiden	litt	gelitten	to suffer
lesen (liest)	las	gelesen	to read
liegen	lag	gelegen	to lie, to be in a horizontal position
lügen	log	gelogen	to tell a lie
mögen (mag)	mochte	mögen (gemocht)	to like
müssen (muß)	mußte	müssen (gemusst)	to have to
nehmen (nimmt)	nahm	genommen	to take
nennen	nannte	genannt	to name
raten (rät)	riet	geraten	to give advice
beraten (berät)	beriet	beraten	to advise (someone)
zerreißen	riß	gerissen	to tear
reißen	zerriß	zerrissen	to tear to shreads
rennen	rannte	gerannt (*S*)	to run
riechen	roch	gerochen	to smell
rufen	rief	gerufen	to call
anrufen	rief ...an	angerufen	to call on the telephone
schlafen (schläft)	schlief	geschlafen	to sleep
schlagen (schlägt)	schlug	geschlagen	to hit
vorschlagen (schlägt ...vor)	schlug ...vor	vorgeschlagen	to suggest
schiessen	schoß	geschossen	to shoot
schließen	schloß	geschlossen	to close
schmelzen (schmilzt)	schmolz	geschmolzen	to melt
schneiden	schnitt	geschnitten	to cut
schreiben	schrieb	geschrieben	to write
beschreiben	beschrieb	beschrieben	to describe
verschreiben	verschrieb	verschrieben	to prescribe
vorschreiben	schrieb ...vor	vorgeschrieben	to require
schreien	schrie	geschrien	to cry, to yell
schwimmen	schwamm	geschwommen	to swim
sehen (sieht)	sah	gesehen	to see
einsehen (sieht...ein)	sah ...ein	eingesehen	to understand, to have insight

Infinitive	Preterite	Past Participle	
sein	war	gewesen (*S*)	to be
singen	sang	gesungen	to sing
sinken	sank	gesunken (*S*)	to sink
sitzen	saß	gesessen	to sit
besitzen	besaß	besessen	to own
sollen (soll)	sollte	sollen (gesollt)	to be obligated to
sprechen (spricht)	sprach	gesprochen	to speak
aussprechen (spricht ...aus)	sprach ...aus	ausgesprochen	to pronounce
besprechen (bespricht)	besprach	besprochen	to discuss
versprechen (verspricht)	versprach	versprochen	to promise
springen	sprang	gesprungen (*S*)	to jump
stehen	stand	gestanden	to stand
aufstehen	stand ...auf	aufgestanden (*S*)	to get up
verstehen	verstand	verstanden	to understand
steigen	stieg	gestiegen (*S*)	to climb
aussteigen	stieg ...aus	ausgestiegen (*S*)	to get out
einsteigen	stieg ...ein	eingestiegen (*S*)	to get in
umsteigen	stieg ...um	umgestiegen (*S*)	to change (planes)
besteigen	bestieg	bestiegen*	to climb a mountain
sterben (stirbt)	starb	gestorben (*S*)	to die
stinken	stank	gestunken	to stink
tragen (trägt)	trug	getragen	to carry, to wear clothes
trinken	trank	getrunken	to drink
ertrinken	ertrank	ertrunken (*S*)	to drown
vergessen (vergisst)	vergaß	vergessen	to forget
verlieren	verlor	verloren	to lose
wachsen (wächst)	wuchs	gewachsen (*S*)	to grow up
waschen (wäscht)	wusch	gewaschen	to wash
werden (wird)	wurde	geworden (*S*)	to become
werfen (wirft)	warf	geworfen	to throw
wiegen	wog	gewogen	to weigh
wissen (weiß)	wußte	gewußt	to know (a fact)
wollen (will)	wollte	wollen (gewollt)	to want to
ziehen	zog	gezogen	to pull
anziehen	zog ...an	angezogen	to put on (clothes)
ausziehen	zog ...aus	ausgezogen	to take off (clothes)
ausziehen	zog ...aus	ausgezogen (*S*)	to move out
einziehen	zog ...ein	eingezogen (*S*)	to move in
umziehen	zog ...um	umgezogen	to change (clothes)
umziehen	zog ...um	umgezogen (*S*)	to move (from one place to another)
zwingen	zwang	gezwungen	to force

Weak Verbs

The following is a list of the most common weak verbs that have prefixes. All other weak verbs follow the regular pattern. (*S* in this list indicates a verb that takes *sein* in its compound tenses.)

Infinitive	Preterite	Past Participle	
antworten	antwortete	geantwortet	to give an answer
beantworten	beantwortete	beantwortet	to answer a question
brauchen	brauchte	gebraucht	to need
gebrauchen	gebrauchte	gebraucht	to use
verbrauchen	verbrauchte	verbraucht	to consume, to use up
decken	deckte	gedeckt	to cover
entdecken	entdeckte	entdeckt	to discover
drucken	druckte	gedruckt	to print
drücken	drückte	gedrückt	to press, to push
ausdrücken	drückte ...aus	ausgedrückt	to express
fordern	forderte	gefordert	to demand
fördern	förderte	gefördert	to support, to further
befördern	beförderte	befördert	to promote someone
führen	führte	geführt	to lead
entführen	entführte	entführt	to abduct
verführen	verführte	verführt	to seduce
holen	holte	geholt	to fetch, to get
abholen	holte ...ab	abgeholt	to pick up
hören	hörte	gehört	to hear, to listen
aufhören	hörte ...auf	aufgehört	to cease, to stop
gehören	gehörte	gehört	to belong to
kaufen	kaufte	gekauft	to buy
verkaufen	verkaufte	verkauft	to sell
leben	lebte	gelebt	to be alive, to live
erleben	erlebte	erlebt	to experience
mieten	mietete	gemietet	to rent
vermieten	vermietete	vermietet	to rent out
sagen	sagte	gesagt	to say, to tell
versagen	versagte	versagt	to fail at something
schalten	schaltete	geschaltet	to operate a switch
abschalten	schaltete ...ab	abgeschaltet	to shut down
ausschalten	schaltete ...aus	ausgeschaltet	to turn off
einschalten	schaltete ...ein	eingeschaltet	to turn on
umschalten	schaltete ...um	umgeschaltet	to switch over
setzen	setzte	gesetzt	to set
besetzen	besetzte	besetzt	to occupy
versetzen	versetzte	versetzt	to transfer (someone)

Infinitive	Preterite	Past Participle	
steigern	steigerte	gesteigerte	to increase
ersteigern	ersteigerte	ersteigert	to win at an auction
versteigern	versteigerte	versteigert	to auction off
stellen	stellte	gestellt	to place upright
bestellen	bestellte	bestellt	to place an order
stören	störte	gestört	to disturb
zerstören	zerstörte	zerstört	to destroy
suchen	suchte	gesucht	to look for
besuchen	besuchte	besucht	to visit
versuchen	versuchte	versucht	to try
teilen	teilte	geteilt	to divide, to share
verteilen	verteilte	verteilt	to distribute
wandern	wanderte	gewandert (*S*)	to hike
auswandern	wanderte ...aus	ausgewandert (*S*)	to emigrate
einwandern	wanderte ...ein	eingewandert (*S*)	to immigrate
warten	wartete	gewartet	to wait
erwarten	erwartete	erwartet	to expect
zahlen	zahlte	gezahlt	to pay
bezahlen	bezahlen	bezahlt	to pay a bill
zählen	zählte	gezählt	to count
erzählen	erzählte	erzählt	to tell a story
zeichnen	zeichnete	gezeichnet	to draw a picture
bezeichnen	bezeichnete	bezeichnet	to characterize

Part Two:
Essentials of Grammar

18. The Article

Nouns and pronouns in German have markers that indicate gender, number, and case. In English only certain pronouns have clear gender, number, and case markings, including "he," "she," "him," "her," and "it." Most English nouns are marked for number, but not for case or gender.

Singular	*Plural*
the book	the books
the boy	the boys
the goose	the geese
the lady	the ladies
the man	the men

German, however, has a complete set of markers for gender, number, and case. These are clearly present on the pronoun, but not always on the noun itself. The definite article, equivalent to English "the," which always precedes the noun, has the endings to distinguish gender, number, and case.

	Masculine	Singular Feminine	Neuter	Plural
Nominative	**der**	**die**	**das**	**die**
Accusative	**den**	**die**	**das**	**die**
Dative	**dem**	**der**	**dem**	**den**
Genitive	**des**	**der**	**des**	**der**

The indefinite article (English "a/an") has the following forms:

	Masculine	Feminine	Neuter
Nominative	**ein**	**eine**	**ein**
Accusative	**einen**	**eine**	**ein**
Dative	**einem**	**einer**	**einem**
Genitive	**eines**	**einer**	**eines**

Gender, number, and case are discussed in detail in Chapter 19, **Nouns.**

19. Nouns

Gender

1. The gender of German nouns is identified by the endings attached to articles and other demonstratives. Grammatical gender in German often has little to do with natural gender (sex). Thus, a noun is replaced by its appropriate pronoun.

Singular

der Tisch*	the table	er	it
die Tasche	the pocket	sie	it
das Tuch	the cloth	es	it

*Note: German nouns are *always* capitalized, no matter what their position in a sentence.

Plural

die Tische	the tables	sie	they
die Taschen	the pockets	sie	they
die Tücher	the cloths	sie	they

The subject pronouns introduced in Chapter 2 illustrate the relation between gender of nouns and gender of pronouns. Note that in the plural no distinction is made as to gender.

2. The gender of German nouns cannot always be determined by its written or spoken form. To English speakers, the gender of German nouns often seems very arbitrary. There are, however, a number of rules that apply to large categories of nouns.

The names of male beings are generally masculine (*der*).

der Mann	man, husband	der Bär	bear
der Hahn	rooster	der Lehrer	teacher (male)
der Hengst	stallion		

The names of female beings are generally feminine (*die*).

die Frau	woman	die Bärin	she-bear
die Henne	hen	die Lehrerin	teacher (female)
die Stute	mare		

All nouns that end in *-chen* or *-lein* are neuter (*das*). There are no exceptions to this rule.

das Männlein	little man	das Fingerchen	small finger
das Fräulein	Miss	das Tischlein	little table

All nouns that end in *-ung, -heit/-keit, -tät, -ei, -erei, -ie,* and *-schaft* are feminine *(die).* There are no exceptions to this rule.

die Übung exercise	**die Melodie** melody
die Schönheit beauty	**die Freundschaft** friendship
die Einigkeit unity	**die Bäckerei** bakery
die Universität university	

The names of the letters of the alphabet are neuter *(das).*

das F in "fein" the F in "fine"   **das ABC** the ABCs

The names of cities are neuter *(das),* although the article is not ordinarily used with place names.

(das) **Berlin**	*(das)* **Paris**
(das) **London**	*(das)* **New York**

The names of *most* countries are neuter *(das).* (Articles are *not* ordinarily used with the names of countries of neuter gender.)

(das) **Deutschland** Germany	*(das)* **Norwegen** Norway
(das) **Amerika** America	*(das)* **Dänemark** Denmark
(das) **Italien** Italy	

The names of the following countries are feminine *(die).* (Articles *must* accompany the names of countries of feminine gender.)

die Schweiz Switzerland	**die Vatikanstadt** Vatican City
die Tschechoslowakei Czechoslovakia	**Die Schweiz ist klein** Switzerland is
die Türkei Turkey	small.
	Die Türkei ist groß. Turkey is large.

The names of most rivers in the German-speaking world are feminine *(die).*

die Elbe the Elbe	**die Havel** the Havel
die Donau the Danube	**die Weser** the Weser
die Isar the Isar	

The following non-German rivers are also feminine *(die).*

die Seine the Seine	**die Wolga** the Volga
die Themse the Thames	**die Weichsel** the Vistula

Most other rivers are masculine *(der)* in analogy with *der Fluß* ("river").

der Rhein	**der Missouri**
der Main	**der Wisconsin**
der Neckar	**der Brahmaputra**
der Mississippi	**der Ganges**

The days of the week, the months and the seasons of the year, as well as all words compounded with *der Tag* (''day'') are masculine *(der)*.

der Mittwoch	Wednesday	**der Herbst**	autumn
der März	March	**der Feiertag**	holiday

Number (Plural)

The plural is formed in a number of ways. Nouns ending in -*e* usually add an -*n*.

die Tasche	**die Taschen**	pocket(s), bag(s), sack(s)
der Kunde	**die Kunden**	customer(s)
das Auge	**die Augen**	eye(s)

Many masculine *(der)* nouns add an -*e:*

der Tisch	**die Tische**	table(s)
der Tag	**die Tage**	day(s)
der Arm	**die Arme**	arm(s)

Most feminine *(die)* nouns add an -*en:*

die Tür	**die Türen**	door(s)
die Uhr	**die Uhren**	clock(s)
die Frau	**die Frauen**	woman (women)

A number of common nouns, both masculine (*der*) and feminine (*die*), add an -*e* and an umlaut to the stem-vowel.

der Stuhl	**die Stühle**	chair(s)
der Zug	**die Züge**	train(s)
der Band	**die Bände**	volume(s) (of a book)
der Kopf	**die Köpfe**	head(s)
der Topf	**die Töpfe**	pot(s)
die Hand	**die Hände**	hand(s)
die Nacht	**die Nächte**	night(s)
die Wand	**die Wände**	wall(s)

Several masculine (*der*) and feminine (*die*) nouns form the plural by adding an umlaut to the stem-vowel.

der Mantel	**die Mäntel**	(over)coat(s)
der Garten	**die Gärten**	garden(s), yard(s)
der Vater	**die Väter**	father(s)
der Bruder	**die Brüder**	brother(s)
die Mutter	**die Mütter**	mother(s)
die Tochter	**die Töchter**	daughter(s)

Most masculine (*der*) and neuter (*das*) nouns ending in *-er* add nothing in the plural.

der Lehrer	die Lehrer	teacher(s)
der Arbeiter	die Arbeiter	worker(s)
das Fenster	die Fenster	window(s)
das Zimmer	die Zimmer	room(s)
das Laster	die Laster	moral vice(s)
der Lastwagen	die Lastwagen	truck(s)

Many common masculine (*der*) nouns referring to people add *-en.**

der Mensch	die Menschen	human being(s)
der Pilot	die Piloten	pilot(s)
der Student	die Studenten	student(s)

Note: With the exception of the dictionary (nominative) form, these nouns take an *-en* ending everywhere, even in the other cases of the singular. See discussion of Case to follow.

All feminine *(die)* nouns derived from the masculine counterpart and ending in *-in* add *-nen:*

die Lehrerin	die Lehrerinnen	teacher(s)
die Studentin	die Studentinnen	student(s), coed(s)
die Arbeiterin	die Arbeiterinnen	worker(s)

Several common masculine (*der*) and neuter (*das*) nouns add an *-er* and an umlaut to the stem-vowel in the plural.

der Mann	die Männer	man (men)
das Buch	die Bücher	book(s)
das Band	die Bänder	bands, ribbons
der Gott	die Götter	god(s)
das Dorf	die Dörfer	village(s)

Case

All German nouns and pronouns have markers that indicate case. There are four cases.

Nominative: the subject, used to identify objects, persons, places, etc. The nominative is the dictionary form of all nouns and pronouns.

| **Das ist** *der Zug/die Fahrkarte/das Gepäck.* | That is the train/the ticket/the luggage. |
| **Das ist** *ein Gepäckträger/eine Kellnerin/ein Kind.* | That is a porter/a waitress/a child. |

Accusative: the direct object of most transitive verbs; also follows the prepositions *bis* (until, up to), *durch* (through), *für* (for), *gegen* (against), *ohne* (without), and *um* (around). Note that accusative forms are exactly the same as nominative forms for feminine (*die*) and neuter (*das*) nouns and their equivalent pronouns.

Ich sehe *den Zug/die Fahrkarte/das Gepäck.*	I see the train/the ticket/the luggage.
Ich beobachte *einen Gepäckträger/ eine Kellnerin/ein Kind.*	I observe a porter/a waitress/a child.

In the plural, the accusative and nominative are also exactly the same.

Ich sehe die Züge/	I see the trains/
die Gepäckträger/	porters/
die Kellnerinnen/	waitresses/
die Kinder.	children.

Dative: the indirect object; also follows the prepositions *ab* (from this point on), *aus* (out of), *außer* (except), *bei* (at), *gegenüber* (opposite), *mit* (with), *nach* (after, towards), *seit* (since), *von* (of, from), and *zu* (to). Also, verbs such as *helfen* (to help), *schaden* (to injure), *zuhören* (to listen to), and a few others require dative objects.

Ich sage *dem Mann/der Frau/dem Kind* **meine Meinung.**	I tell the man/the woman/the child my opinion.
Ich gebe *einem Gepäckträger/einer Kellnerin* **ein Trinkgeld.**	I give a porter/a waitress a tip.
Ich helfe *dem Kind.*	I help the child.

Genitive: the possessive case; also follows the prepositions (*an*) *statt* (instead of), *trotz* (in spite of), *während* (during), *wegen* (because of), *innerhalb* (inside of), *außerhalb* (outside of), *oberhalb* (above), *unterhalb* (below).

Was ist der Preis *des (eines) Kugelschreibers/der (einer) Fahrkarte/des (eines) Buches?*	What is the price of the (of a) pen/of the (of a) ticket/of the (of a) book?

20. Prepositions

Like English, German has more than one hundred prepositions. In practice, however, only about two dozen are commonly used. German prepositions govern the accusative, dative, and genitive cases.

Accusative

The following prepositions always govern the accusative case:

bis	until, up to	**gegen**	against
durch	through	**ohne**	without
für	for	**um**	around (place); at (clock time)

Es ist schwer für dich.   It is hard for you.
Er baut einen Zaun um den Garten.   He is building a fence around the yard.

Note: *Bis* is rarely used in such a way as to reveal the accusative.

von Montag *bis* **Mittwoch**   from Monday to Wednesday
bis **morgen**   until tomorrow
von zehn *bis* **hundert**   from ten to a hundred

Bis is frequently found linked with *zu* (plus dative), *auf* (plus accusative), *an* (plus accusative), or *nach* (plus dative).

bis **zum nächsten Mal**	until the next time
bis **auf mich**	with the exception of me
bis **ans Ende der Welt**	to the end of the world
bis **nach dem Spiel**	until after the game

Dative

The following prepositions always govern the dative case:

aus   out of
außer   except
bei   in the presence/home/business of
dank   thanks to
gegenüber   opposite, across from
mit   with
nach   to (with place names); after (in sequential order); according to
seit   since
von   of, from, by (passive agent)
zu   to

Von **wem hast du die Blumen?**	Who did you get the flowers from?
Ich habe die Blumen *von* **dem Herrn Gerlach.**	I got the flowers from Mr. Gerlach.

Genitive

The following prepositions usually govern the genitive:

(an)statt instead of	**angesichts** considering
trotz in spite of	**außerhalb** outside (of)
während during	**innerhalb** inside (of)
wegen because of	**oberhalb** above
bezüglich with reference to	**unterhalb** beneath, below
hinsichtlich with regard to	

(an)statt des Weines	instead of the wine
(an)statt meiner	instead of me
wegen des schlechten Wetters	because of the bad weather
wegen deiner	because of you

Formal written German requires the genitive with these prepositions. The informal spoken language, however, frequently uses them with the dative.

(an) statt mir	instead of me
wegen dir	because of you

Accusative/Dative

The following prepositions are frequently called *two-way prepositions* (in German: *Wechselpräpositionen*). They govern the dative when they indicate location in space or time. They govern the accusative when they indicate change of location. They usually govern the accusative when location or change of location is not literally implied by the verb.

Preposition	Dative	Accusative
an	at a vertical surface	towards a vertical surface
auf	on a horizontal surface	onto a horizontal surface
hinter	behind	going behind
in	in	into
neben	next to	moving next to
über	above	crossing over
unter	underneath	moving beneath; going under
vor	in front of, ago (with time)	crossing in front of
zwischen	in between	moving into the area between

Der Student kommt *in* das Zimmer. (accusative)	The student comes into the room.
Der Student sitzt zwei Stunden *im (in dem)* Zimmer. (dative)	The student sits for two hours in the room.
Der Student spricht *über das* Zimmer. (accusative)	The student is talking about the room.

Verbs of motion, such as *gehen, fahren, fallen, reisen,* and *kommen,* will often require one of these prepositions with the accusative.

Wir fahren *in* das Land der Belgier (nach Belgien). (accusative)	We are going to the land of the Belgians (to Belgium).
Wir besuchen Freunde *in* dem Land. (dative)	We are visiting friends in the land.
Er steigt *auf* den Berg. (accusative)	He is climbing (onto) the mountain.
Er steht *auf* dem Berg. (dative)	He is standing on the mountain.

Three pairs of verbs, *liegen/legen, sitzen/setzen,* and *stehen/stellen,* illustrate the difference between the dative and accusative use of these prepositions. The first verb in each pair indicates location, the second indicates change of location. *Liegen/legen* indicates location or horizontal movement, *sitzen/setzen* indicates sitting/setting, *stehen/stellen* indicates location or vertical movement.

Sie *legt* das Buch auf den Tisch.	She is putting the book on(to) the table.
Das Buch *liegt* auf dem Tisch.	The book is (lying) on the table.
Er *stellt* die Lampe in die Ecke.	He is putting (standing up) the lamp in(to) the corner.
Die Lampe *steht* in der Ecke.	The lamp is (standing) in the corner.

Note: *Liegen, sitzen,* and *stehen* are strong verbs. *Legen, setzen,* and *stellen* are weak verbs.

Contractions

A number of prepositions contract with the definite article that follows them.

an + dem	**am**	**am Montag, am Fenster**	on Monday, at the window
bei + dem	**beim**	**beim Friseur**	at the barber shop
in + dem	**im**	**im Zimmer**	in the room
in + das	**ins**	**ins Zimmer**	into the room
für + das	**fürs**	**fürs Baby**	for the baby
um + ums	**ums**	**ums Herz**	around the heart
von + dem	**vom**	**vom Bahnhof**	from the railroad station
zu + dem	**zum**	**zum Beispiel**	for example
zu + der	**zur**	**zur Post**	to the post office

These contractions are usually not separated except for emphasis.

am **Dienstag**	on Tuesday
an **dem Dienstag**	on that particular Tuesday
Du warst *beim* **Friseur.**	You were at the barber.
Du warst *bei dem* **Friseur!**	You were at that barber!

21. Adjectives and Adverbs

In German, adjectives and adverbs have many things in common. They have no characteristic form, unlike many English adverbs that have an "-ly" ending, as in "a quick bite" vs. "the dog runs quickly." They can, in most cases, be marked to indicate comparative or superlative degree. Compare English "more beautiful," "most beautiful" with "beautifully," "more beautifully," "most beautifully." They also modify other parts of speech. (Adjectives modify nouns; adverbs modify verbs, adjectives, and other adverbs.)

German adjectives, however, take endings that reflect gender, number, and case, like nouns. However, this happens only when they appear *before* the noun, not after it. Adjectives also have markers for comparative and superlative degree. German adverbs are marked only for comparative and superlative.

Adjectives

1. When an adjective follows a noun in a sentence, it has no special endings.

Das Buch ist blau.	The book is blue.
Der Bleistift ist gelb.	The pencil is yellow.
Die Tasche ist schwarz.	The bag is black.

When placed in front of the noun, however, adjectives take endings corresponding to gender, number, and case. The basic rule is: If there is no word like *der/die/das* or *ein/eine* present, the adjective(s) take(s) the ending regularly assigned to the *der/die/das* or *ein/eine* word:

blaues Buch	blue book
gelber Bleistift	yellow pencil
schwarze Tasche	black bag

2. The endings for the definite article, presented in Chapter 18, are the same as the endings on the adjectives.

	Masculine	Singular Feminine	Neuter	Plural
Nominative	**der**	**die**	**das**	**die**
Accusative	**den**	**die**	**das**	**die**
Dative	**dem**	**der**	**dem**	**den**
Genitive	**des**	**der**	**des**	**der**

Separated out, the endings look like this:

	Masculine	Singular Feminine	Neuter	Plural
Nominative	-r	-e	-s	-e
Accusative	-n	-e	-s	-e
Dative	-m	-r	-m	-n
Genitive	-s(n*)	-r	-s(n*)	-r

*Note: Unpreceded adjectives in the genitive singular masculine and neuter have an -*n* instead of the -*s* that one would expect.

Was ist der Preis des roten Weines? What is the price of the red wine?
Was ist der Preis *roten* (not *rotes*) **Weines?** What is the price of red wine?

good wine	good milk	good bread	good friends
guter Wein	**gute Milch**	**gutes Brot**	**gute Freunde**
guten Wein	**gute Milch**	**gutes Brot**	**gute Freunde**
gutem Wein	**guter Milch**	**gutem Brot**	**guten Freunden**
guten Weines	**guter Milch**	**guten Brotes**	**guter Freunde**

3. When an adjective is preceded by an article or a word like an article (*der/die/das, ein/eine,* etc.), the adjectives take slightly different endings.

	Masculine	Singular Feminine	Neuter	Plural
Nominative	-e(r)	-e	-e(s)	-en
Accusative	-en	-e	-e(s)	-en
Dative	-en	-en	-en	-en
Genitive	-en	-en	-en	-en

the good wine	the good milk	the good bread	the good friends
der gute Wein	**die gute Milch**	**das gute Brot**	**die guten Freunde**
den guten Wein	**die gute Milch**	**das gute Brot**	**die guten Freunde**
dem guten Wein	**der guten Milch**	**dem guten Brot**	**den guten Freunden**
des guten Weines	**der guten Milch**	**des guten Brotes**	**der guten Freunde**

no good wine	no good milk	no good bread	no good friends
kein guter Wein	**keine gute Milch**	**kein gutes Brot**	**keine guten Freunde**
keinen guten Wein	**keine gute Milch**	**kein gutes Brot**	**keine guten Freunde**
keinem guten Wein	**keiner guten Milch**	**keinem guten Brot**	**keinen guten Freunden**
keines guten Weines	**keiner guten Milch**	**keinem guten Brot**	**keiner guten Freunde**

Comparison of Adjectives and Adverbs

1. All adjectives and adverbs have endings that indicate comparative ("more") and superlative ("most") degree.

Comparative: **-er(-)**   Superlative: **-st(-)**

2. In the case of adjectives, the resulting forms are new adjectives that take the same endings as regular adjectives.

schön	beautiful	schöner	more beautiful	schönst-	most beautiful
klein	small	kleiner	smaller	kleinst-	smallest
dick	fat	dicker	fatter	dickst-	fattest

Multisyllabic adjectives form their comparative and superlative forms in the same way.

interessant	interesting	interessanter	more interesting	interessantest	most interesting
beliebt	beloved	beliebter	more beloved	beliebtest	most beloved
ausgezeichnet	excellent	ausgezeichneter	more excellent	ausgezeichnetest	most excellent

3. The *superlative* form as illustrated here cannot be used alone. It is possible to say:

Positive:
Dieses Buch ist klein.   This book is small.

Comparative:
Das Buch da ist kleiner.   That book is smaller.

But you must say:

Superlative:
Das ist das kleinste Buch.   That is the smallest book.

If, however, the superlative does not precede the noun, as in the last example above, either one of two ways of expressing the superlative adjective is possible. First of all, one can use the article plus the appropriate adjective *without* the noun. (English normally replaces the noun in question with the word "one(s).")

Das Buch ist das *kleinste* (Buch).   The book is the smallest (book) one.
Der Tisch ist der *teuerste* (Tisch). The table is the most expensive (table) one.
Die Alpen sind die *schönsten* (Berge). The Alps are the most beautiful (mountains) ones.

It is also possible to express the superlative by using *am ...-sten.*

Das Buch ist *am* klein*sten.*   The book is the smallest.
Der Tisch ist *am* teuer*sten.*   The table is the most expensive.
Die Bluse ist *am* neue*sten.*   The blouse is the newest.
Die Alpen sind *am* schön*sten.*   The Alps are the most beautiful.

Adverbs

Adverbs like *hier* ("here"), *dort* ("there"), *jetzt* ("now"), *nie* ("never"), *sehr* ("very"), *ziemlich* ("quite," "rather"), etc., are like their English counterparts. Adjectives that function like adverbs, such as *schön* ("beautifully"), *schnell* ("quickly"), *ruhig* ("peacefully"), *gut* ("well"), and *schlecht* ("poorly," "badly") can be marked for comparative and superlative just like adjectives. However, only the form marked *am...-sten* can be used for adverbs in the superlative.

schnell, schneller, am schnellsten	fast, faster, fastest
schlecht, schlechter, am schlechtesten	bad, worse, worst
freundlich, freundlicher, am freundlichsten	friendly, friendlier, friendliest

Irregular Adjectives and Adverbs

alt, älter, ältest-/am ältesten	old, older, oldest
arm, ärmer, ärmest-/am ärmsten	poor, poorer, poorest
bald, eher, am ehesten (adverb only)	soon, sooner, soonest
dumm, dümmer, dümmst-/am dümmsten	dumb, dumber, dumbest
gut, besser, best-/am besten	good (well), better, best
hart, härter, härtest	hard, harder, hardest
jung, jünger, jüngst-/am jüngsten	young, younger, youngest
rot, röter, rötest-/am rötesten	red, redder, reddest
schwach, schwächer, schwächst-/am schwächsten	weak, weaker, weakest
schwarz, schwärzer, schwärzest-/am schwärzesten	black, blacker, blackest
klug, klüger, klügst-/am klügsten	smart, smarter, smartest
lang, länger, längst-/am längsten	long, longer, longest
kurz, kürzer, kürzest-/am kürzesten	short, shorter, shortest
stark, stärker, stärkst-/am stärksten	strong, stronger, strongest
gesund, gesünder, gesündest-/am gesündesten	healthy, healthier, healthiest
groß, größer, größt-/am größten	big/great, bigger/greater, biggest/greatest
hoch, höher, höchst-/am höchsten	high/tall, higher/taller, highest/tallest
nah, näher, nächst-/am nächsten	near, nearer, nearest
kalt, kälter, kältest-/am kältesten	cold, colder, coldest
warm, wärmer, wärmst-/am wärmsten	warm, warmer, warmest

Gern

The irregular adverb *gern* is used to indicate a liking or preference for a particular activity.

gern, lieber, am liebsten*

Gern makes a verb into the equivalent of "like to."

Ich schreibe Briefe.	I write letters.
Ich schreibe gern Briefe.	I like to write letters.
Er arbeitete dort.	He worked there.
Er arbeitete gern dort.	He liked to work there.
Wir wären gekommen.	We would have come.
Wir wären gern gekommen.	We would have gladly come.

Lieber indicates the equivalent of "prefer to."

Er schreibt gern, aber er liest lieber.	He likes to write but he prefers to read.
Wir wären gern gekommen, aber wir hätten euch lieber zu uns eingeladen.	We would have liked to come, but we would have preferred to invite you over to our place.

Am liebsten means "most of all."

Ich trinke Cola gern, Bier lieber, aber Wein am liebsten.	I like to drink Coke, prefer beer, but like wine most of all.
W.C. Fields wäre am liebsten in Philadelphia gewesen.	W.C. Fields would have liked being in Philadelphia most of all.

*Note: *Gern* should not be confused with *lieb,* meaning "dear," "kind," "nice," which has the same comparative and superlative forms, *lieber, liebst-/am liebsten,* but which is an adjective, not an adverb.

22. Numbers

Numbers are adjectives that normally do not take any endings. The notable exception is *ein*, which means "one" or "a/an." It takes the same endings as *kein/keine*, which was illustrated in the previous chapter.

	Masculine	Feminine	Neuter
Nominative	**ein**	**eine**	**ein**
Accusative	**einen**	**eine**	**ein**
Dative	**einem**	**einer**	**einem**
Genitive	**eines**	**einer**	**eines**

Cardinal Numbers

1. The cardinal numbers in German are as follows.

0	**null** zero	
1	**eins** one	
2	**zwei** two	
3	**drei** three	
4	**vier** four	
5	**fünf** five	
6	**sechs** six	
7	**sieben** seven	
8	**acht** eight	
9	**neun** nine	
10	**zehn** ten	
11	**elf** eleven	
12	**zwölf** twelve	
13	**dreizehn** thirteen	
14	**vierzehn** fourteen	
15	**fünfzehn** fifteen	
16	**sechszehn** sixteen	
17	**siebzehn** seventeen	
18	**achtzehn** eighteen	
19	**neunzehn** nineteen	
20	**zwanzig** twenty	
21	**einundzwanzig** twenty-one	
22	**zweiundzwanzig** twenty-two	
23	**dreiundzwanzig** twenty-three	
24	**vierundzwanzig** twenty-four	
25	**fünfundzwanzig** twenty-five	
26	**sechsundzwanzig** twenty-six	
27	**siebenundzwanzig** twenty-seven	
28	**achtundzwanzig** twenty-eight	
29	**neunundzwanzig** twenty-nine	
30	**dreißig** thirty	

31	**einunddreißig** thirty-one
40	**vierzig** forty
42	**zweiundvierzig** forty-two
50	**fünfzig** fifty
53	**dreiundfünfzig** fifty-three
60	**sechzig** sixty
64	**vierundsechzig** sixty-four
70	**siebzig** seventy
75	**fünfundsiebzig** seventy-five
80	**achtzig** eighty
86	**sechsundachtzig** eighty-six
90	**neunzig** ninety
97	**siebenundneunzig** ninety-seven
100	**(ein)hundert** one hundred
108	**(ein)hundertacht** one hundred and eight
200	**zweihundert** two hundred
209	**zweihundertneun** two hundred and nine
900	**neunhundert** nine hundred
1.000	**tausend** one thousand
3.000	**dreitausend** three thousand
1.000.000	**eine Million** one million
8.000.000	**acht Millionen** eight million
1.000.000.000	**eine Milliarde** one billion
4.000.000.000	**vier Milliarden** four billion
1.000.000.000.000	**eine Billion** one trillion

The numbers not listed follow the pattern set up for the numbers between *zwanzig* and *dreißig*.

2. Large numbers are usually written with a space or a period (.) where English uses a comma (,), and with a comma where English uses a period. Thus, 158,497.62 is written in German as either 158 497,62 or 158.497,62. It is read in German *hundertachtundfünfzigtausend vierhundertsiebenundneunzig Komma zweiundsechzig.*

3. The names of cardinal numbers can be used as nouns. They are feminine (*die*) when so used:

die Eins   the (number) one   **die Zehn**   the (number) ten
die Sechs   the (number) six   **die Hundert**   the (number) hundred

Ordinal Numbers

1. The ordinal numbers in German are as follows.

erst-	first	**einundzwanzigst-**	twenty-first
zweit-	second	**zweiundzwanzigst-**	twenty-second
dritt-	third	**dreiundzwanzigst-**	twenty-third
viert-	fourth	**vierundzwanzigst-**	twenty-fourth
fünft-	fifth	**fünfundzwanzigst-**	twenty-fifth
sechst-	sixth	**sechsundzwanzigst-**	twenty-sixth
siebt-	seventh	**siebenundzwanzigst-**	twenty-seventh
acht-	eighth	**achtundzwanzigst-**	twenty-eighth
neunt-	ninth	**neunundzwanzigst-**	twenty-ninth
zehnt-	tenth	**dreißigst-**	thirtieth
elft-	eleventh	**einunddreißigst-**	thirty-first
zwölft-	twelfth	**vierzigst-**	fortieth
dreizehnt-	thirteenth	**fünfzigst-**	fiftieth
vierzehnt-	fourteenth	**sechzigst-**	sixtieth
fünfzehnt-	fifteenth	**siebzigst-**	seventieth
sechzehnt-	sixteenth	**achtzigst-**	eightieth
siebzehnt-	seventeenth	**neunzigst-**	ninetieth
achtzehnt-	eighteenth	**hundertest-**	hundredth
neunzehnt-	nineteenth	**tausendst-**	thousandth
zwanzigst-	twentieth	**letzt-**	last

2. Like other adjectives, ordinal numbers take endings that indicate gender, number, and case.

der erst*e* Mensch   the first human being
mein dritt*es* Wörterbuch   my third dictionary
zum fünfzehnt*en* Mal   for the fifteenth time

3. When ordinals are written as numerals, they are always followed by a period (.).

Heute ist der 18. Juli.	Today is the 18th of July.
In diesem Jahr feiern wir den 208.	This year we are celebrating the 208th
Geburtstag der USA.	birthday of the USA.

4. When indicating the order of accession to a royal throne or nobility of birth, German uses the given name followed by the ordinal number with appropriate endings for gender and case:

Wilhelm II. = Wilhelm der Zweite	William II/William the Second
Ich kenne Wilhelm den Zweiten.	I know William the Second.
Er war ein Freund von Wilhelm dem Zweiten.	He was a friend of William the Second.
Das ist das Schloß Wilhelms des Zweiten.	That is William the Second's castle.

Fractions

In reading fractions, the numerator is a cardinal number ("one," *ein*). The denominator is an ordinal number with the ending *-el*. The result is a phrase with a number and a noun that does *not* change form when it becomes plural.

ein Drittel	1/3
zwei Drittel	2/3
ein Viertel	1/4
zwei Fünftel	2/5
sechs Zwanzigstel	6/20
dreizehn Neununddreißigstel	13/39
siebenundfünfzig Einhundertneunundneunzigstel	57/199

"One half" is *eine Hälfte* (plural, *Hälften*). "Half of" is *die Hälfte von* or *die Hälfte* followed by the genitive. "A half (of) a(n)" is *ein(e) halbe(r)(s)*.

eine Hälfte der Gruppe	one half of the group
beide Hälften der Kugel	both halves of the ball (sphere)
die Hälfte der Studenten	half of the students
die Hälfte vom (von dem) Kuchen	half of the cake
ein halbes Hähnchen	a half a chicken
eine halbe Zwiebel	a half an onion

With other numbers, "and a half" is *einhalb*.

zweieinhalb	2 1/2
fünfeinhalb	5 1/2

"One and a half" (1 1/2) is *anderthalb* or *eineinhalb*.

Arithmetic

+ (das **Pluszeichen**) *plus* (the plus sign) **plus**

$2 + 3 = 5$ **zwei** *plus* **drei gleicht (ist, macht) fünf**
$9 + 6 = 15$ **neun** *plus* **sechs gleicht (ist, macht) fünfzehn**

− (das **Minuszeichen**) *minus, weniger* (the minus sign) **minus, less**

$16 − 9 = 7$ **sechszehn** *minus* **neun ist (gleicht, macht) sieben**
$8 − 8 = 0$ **acht** *minus* **acht ist (gleicht, macht) null**

× (das **Multiplikationszeichen**) *mal* (the multiplication sign) **times**

$5 \times 3 = 15$ **fünf** *mal* **drei macht (gleicht, ist) fünfzehn**
$6 \times 4 = 24$ **sechs** *mal* **vier macht (gleicht, ist) vierundzwanzig**

÷ (das **Divisionszeichen**) *geteilt durch* (the division sign) **divided by**

$9 \div 3 = 3$ **neun** *geteilt* **durch drei ist drei**
$30 \div 6 = 5$ **dreißig** *geteilt* **durch sechs ist fünf**

= (das **Gleichzeichen**) *gleicht (ist, macht)* (the equal sign) **equals**

23. Demonstrative Adjectives

Demonstrative adjectives indicate information such as location, number, and quality. They correspond to the English "this," "that," "those," "each," "all," "which," "such a(n)," etc. Most German demonstrative adjectives are inflected for gender, number, and case. They can be used either alone or in front of the noun in question. In the lists that follow, singular forms are separated from plural forms by a double slash (//).

der, die, das//die	the; that//those*
dieser, diese, dieses//diese	this//these
welcher, welche, welches//welche	which (one//ones)?
mancher, manche, manches//manche	many a(n)//many
jeder, jede, jedes	each, every (no plural)
alles//alle	everything, all//all, all of
so ein, so eine, so ein//solche**	such a(n)//such...like that//those
viel***	much of something, a lot of something
vieles	much, a lot (pronoun)
viele	many, a lot of things, people, ideas, etc.
einige	a few, some
wenig***	little, not much
wenige	few, not many
mehrere	several
mehr***	more (of an object or objects)
weniger	less
etwas***	something, some
jemand	someone, somebody
irgendein, irgendeine//irgenwelche	any (at all)
der meiste, die meiste, das meiste//die meisten	most (of the)

*Note: Although the older word *jener, jene, jenes//jene* is still found in written German, it is rarely used in modern spoken German. To distinguish between "this" and "that" in German use *dieser, diese, dieses//diese* for "this//these" and *der, die, das//die* (intensified by a word such as *da* or *dort* ("there")) for "that//those." **Meinst du dieses Buch (hier) oder das Buch (dort drüben)?** Do you mean this book (here) or that book (over there)?

***Solcher, solche, solches//solche* is also possible.

***Mehr and *etwas* are not inflected. *Viel* and *wenig* are inflected only when they are used in an adjective phrase.

Viel Wein kostet viel Geld.	A lot of wine costs a lot of money.
Mit dem vielen Wein kann man sich gut betrinken	With that much wine you can get very drunk.

Das

The pronoun *das* is a universal demonstrative. It is often used without reference to gender or number. It can be translated as "that//those" or "this//these."

Was ist das?	What is that (this)?
Das ist ein Tisch.	That is a table
Das ist eine Tasche.	That is a bag.
Das ist ein Fenster.	That is a window.
Was sind das?	What are those (these) things?
Das sind Tische.	Those (These) are tables.
Wer ist das?	Who is that?
Das ist mein Onkel.	That is my uncle.

24. Possessive Adjectives and Pronouns

Possessive adjectives operate much like demonstrative adjectives, in that they can 1) stand alone (like pronouns) or 2) be placed in front of their respective noun. As a result, there are really two sets of related forms, one for use in front of the noun and one for use alone. In the lists below, the singular and plural forms are separated by a double slash (//). Possessive adjectives and pronouns are inflected for gender, number, and case. (See *kein*, p. 74, and *ein*, p. 78.)

The following forms are used before adjectives and nouns.

mein, meine, mein//meine	my_____
dein, deine, dein//deine	your_____
sein, seine, sein//seine	his_____, its_____
ihr (Ihr), ihr (Ihre), ihr (Ihr)//ihre (Ihre)	her_____, their_____, (your_____)
unser, unsere, unser//unsere	our_____
euer, eu(e)re, euer//eu(e)re	your_____

The following forms are used alone as pronouns.

meiner, meine, meines//meine	mine
deiner, deine, deines//deine	yours
seiner, seine//seines//seine	his
ihrer (Ihrer), ihre (Ihre), ihres (Ihres)//ihre (Ihre)	hers, theirs, (yours)
unserer, unsere, unseres//unsere	ours
eu(e)rer, eu(e)re, eu(e)res//eu(e)re	yours

25. Object Pronouns

1. Subject pronouns were introduced in Chapter 2. All personal pronouns have forms that indicate the accusative, dative, and genitive. The object pronouns are

	Singular		Plural	
Nominative:	**ich**	I	**wir**	we
Accusative:	**mich**	me	**uns**	us
Dative:	**mir**	to me	**uns**	to us
Genitive:	**meiner***	of me	**unser***	of us
Nominative:	**du**	you	**ihr**	you
Accusative:	**dich**	you	**euch**	you
Dative:	**dir**	to you	**euch**	to you
Genitive:	**deiner***	of you	**euer***	of you
Nominative:	**er**	he	**sie**	they
	sie	she	**es**	it
Accusative:	**ihn**	him	**sie**	them
	sie	her	**es**	it
Dative:	**ihm**	to him	**ihnen**	to them
	ihr	to her	**ihm**	to it
Genitive:	**seiner***		**ihrer***	
	ihrer*		**seiner***	

*Note: The genitive pronouns are rarely used in modern German.

2. The objcct pronouns are used in exactly the same way as corresponding nouns, with one qualification. After a preposition, a pronoun is normally used only if it refers to a person.

für mich	for me
mit dir	with you
außer ihm	except for him
bei ihr	at her place
ohne sie	without her/them
von uns	from/of us

3. When the pronoun idea involved refers to an inanimate object, a compound involving the word *da-* (*dar-* preceding a vowel) is used.

auf dem Tisch   on the table
darauf   on it

in der Tasche   in the pocket
darin   in it

vor der Schule   in front of the school
davor   in front (of it)

hinter den Häusern   behind the houses
dahinter   behind them

zwischen dem Haus und der Schule   between the house and the school
dazwischen   between (them)

4. Each *da-/dar-*word has a corresponding question form with *wo-? (wor-?* before a vowel).

Worüber **sprechen Sie heute?**	What are you speaking about today?
Ich sprechen über die Inflation in	I am speaking about inflation in
Argentinien.	Argentina.
Ich spreche *darüber.*	I am speaking about it.
Woran **denkst du?**	What are you thinking about?
Ich denke an einen Tag in Mai.	I am thinking about a day in May.
Ich denke *daran.*	I am thinking about it.

5. Note that not every preposition plus pronoun can be replaced by a *da-/dar-*compound. The prepositions below are replaced by the following compounds listed in boldface.

ohne	**ohne, ohnedies** ("without it")
bis	**bis dahin** ("until then")
außer	**außerdem** ("besides" "in addition")
seit	**seitdem** ("since" as an adverb)
statt	**stattdessen** ("instead")
trotz	**trotzdem** ("nevertheless")
während	**währenddessen** ("in the meanwhile")
wegen	**deswegen** ("for that reason")

6. In addition to the pronouns above, the articles *der/die/das* are frequently used as pronouns, as substitutes for *er/sie/es.* This renders the pronoun idea emphatic.

Der **kann gut reden!**	*He* should talk!
Was gibst du mir für *die?*	What will you give me for *them?*
Die **sieht aber gut aus!**	Does *she* ever look good!

7. Note that the pronouns always take the case appropriate to the sentence, even if the sentence is incomplete.

Wer ist da?	Who is there?
Ich (bin es)!	Me (lit.: I am it)!
Wen meinst du?	Who(m) do you mean?
Dich (meine ich)!	You (I mean)!
Wer soll gehen?	Who is supposed to go?
Du (sollst gehen)!	You (are supposed to go)!
Wem gibst du das Geld?	To whom are you giving the money?
Mir!	(To) Me!
Wer ist gekommen?	Who came?
Er!	He did!

26. Reflexive Pronouns

1. The term *reflexive* refers to a situation in which the subject and one of the objects in a sentence are the same. English has reflexives:

I saw *myself* in the mirror.
She talks to *herself* all the time.
He buys *himself* only the best clothes.
We cannot imagine *ourselves* living anywhere else.

2. The object pronouns discussed in the previous chapter also serve as reflexive pronouns.

Nominative:	**ich**	I	**wir**	we
Accusative:	**mich**	myself	**uns**	ourselves
Dative:	**mir**	to myself	**uns**	to ourselves
Genitive:	**meiner**	of myself	**unser**	of ourselves*

Nominative:	**du**	you	**ihr**	you
Accusative:	**dich**	yourself	**euch**	yourselves
Dative:	**dir**	to yourself	**euch**	to yourselves
Genitive:	**deiner**	of yourself	**euer**	of yourselves*

Ich sehe *mich* im Spiegel.	I see myself in the mirror.
Wir sehen *uns* jeden Tag.	We see each other every day.

*Note: See note in Chapter 25 about the use of the genitive.

In the third person, singular and plural, as well as for *Sie,* a single pronoun is used for reflexive constructions, namely *sich.*

Er fragt *sich* das oft.	He often asks himself that.
Sie kaufen *sich* Wein.	They/You buy themselves/yourself (yourselves) wine.

3. If a verb can take an object, it usually *must* take one, even if the object must be reflexive. As a result, there are many reflexive verbs in German whose counterparts in English are not reflexive.

erinnern (an + accusative)	to remind (of)
sich erinnern (an + accusative)	to remember
interessiern (für + accusative)	to interest (in)
sich interessieren (für + accusative)	to be interested (in)

einigen	to unite two opinions
sich einigen (über + accusative)	to agree (about)
finden	to find
sich befinden	to be located
fühlen	to feel (touch) something
sich fühlen	to feel a certain emotion or sensation
fragen	to ask
sich fragen	to wonder (to ask oneself)
lieben	to love
sich verlieben (in + accusative)	to fall in love (with)
wundern	to amaze
sich wundern	to be amazed

27. Relative Pronouns

1. The relative pronouns in English are "that," "who," "whom," "whose," and "which."

> Who was that man (*whom*) I saw you with last night?
> These are the times *that* try men's souls.
> Have you seen the new film (*that is*) playing in town?

2. German has a complete set of relative pronouns, with forms for gender, number, and case. The relative pronouns are basically the definite article *der/die/das* with some minor modifications in the genitive and dative cases.

	Singular			Plural
	Masculine	Feminine	Neuter	
Nominative:	**der**	**die**	**das**	**die**
Accusative:	**den**	**die**	**das**	**die**
Dative:	**dem**	**der**	**dem**	**denen**
Genitive:	**dessen**	**deren**	**dessen**	**deren**

3. In selecting the appropriate relative pronoun, the gender and number are determined by the gender and number of the antecedent (the word referred back to in the first sentence). The case is determined by the case of the word in the second sentence.

Das Buch ist schwarz.	The book is black.
Das Buch liegt auf dem Tisch.	The book is lying on the table.
Das Buch, *das* auf dem Tisch liegt, ist schwarz.	The book that is (lying) on the table is black.
Der Stuhl steht am Fenster.	The chair is in front of the window.
Ich sehe den Stuhl.	I see the table.
Der Stuhl, *den* ich sehe, steht am Fenster.	The chair that I see is in front of the window.
Die Tasche kostet zu viel.	The purse costs too much.
Ich gebe Ihnen zwei Mark für die Tasche.	I'll give you two Marks for the purse.
Die Tasche, *für die* ich Ihnen zwei Mark gebe, kostet zuviel.	The purse that I'll give you two Marks for, costs too much.
Der Student heißt Markus.	The student is named Markus.
Seine Noten sind gut.	His grades are good.
Der Student, *dessen* Noten gut sind, heißt Markus.	The student whose grades are good is named Markus.

Note: *Dessen/deren* are usually translated as "whose."

Die Bücher, *deren* **Umschläge aus Leder sind, sind sehr alt.**	The books *whose* covers are (made) of leather are very old.
Der Mann, *dessen* **Auto kaputt ist, weint.**	The man *whose* car is wrecked is crying.

4. The verb after a relative pronoun goes at the end of its clause, and the relative pronoun is placed at the front of the clause. If the relative pronoun is part of a prepositional phrase, the preposition stays in front of its pronoun. In such cases, the relative pronoun *must* be used. It cannot be left out, as is often the case in English.

Wer war die Frau, mit der ich dich gestern abend gesehen habe?	Who was that woman (whom) I saw you with last night?
Wie heißt der Roman, den du mir empfohlen hast?	What is the name of that novel (that) you told me to read?
Das ist ein Film, den du sehen sollst.	That is a film (that) you ought to see.
Hier ist das Zimmer, das Sie am Telefon reserviert haben.	Here is the room (that) you reserved over the phone.

28. Negatives

Nicht

1. The most common negative in German is *nicht* ("not"). It is placed *after* a verb, but normally *before* other parts of speech.

Meine Uhr geht *nicht.*	My watch does not work.
Es ist *nicht* **meine Uhr.**	It is not my watch.
Meine Uhr ist *nicht* **alt.**	My watch is not old.
Deine Uhr funktioniert *nicht* **besonders gut.**	Your watch does not function especially well.

2. The placement of *nicht* is otherwise determined by the emphasis the speaker or writer wishes to give an utterance.

Er ist heute abend *nicht* **zu Hause.**	He is not home this evening.
Wir waren vorigen Sommer *nicht* **in Chicago.**	We were not in Chicago last summer.

It is also possible for *nicht* to be the last element in a simple sentence. Normally *nicht* will follow an expression of time but precede an expression of place.

Die Studenten studieren heutzutage *nicht.*	(The) students do not study nowadays.
Die Studenten studieren *nicht* **in der Universität.**	(The) students do not study in the university.

3. *Nicht* is found at the beginning of a sentence only if it modifies a (pro)noun or adjective or adverb already there. It cannot stand alone at the beginning of a sentence.

Nicht **ich, sondern wir, gehen.**	Not I, but we, are going.
Nicht **rot, sondern schwarz, war das Telefon.**	Not red, but black, was the telephone.

Kein/keine

Most nouns are negated by means of the demonstrative adjective *kein/keine,* which is inflected exactly like *mein/meine, dein/deine, sein/seine,* and *ihr/ihre (Ihr/Ihre).*

		Singular		Plural
	Masculine	Feminine	Neuter	
Nominative:	**kein**	**keine**	**kein**	**keine**
Accusative:	**keinen**	**keine**	**kein**	**keine**
Dative:	**keinem**	**keiner**	**keinem**	**keinen**
Genitive:	**keines**	**keiner**	**keines**	**keiner**

Kein/keine corresponds to English "not a(n), not any, no..."

Nein, ich haben *keinen* (Bleistift). No, I do not (have a pencil).
Es gibt *keine* Wolken am Himmel. There are no clouds in the sky.
Das sind *keine* Wolken, das ist Nebel. Those are not clouds, that is fog.

Other Negatives

In addition to *nicht* and *kein/keine* there are a number of pronouns and adverbs that carry a negative meaning:

nichts   nothing
niemand   nobody, no one
nirgends   nowhere

nirgendwohin   (to) nowhere
nie   never

Ich gehe *nie* ins Kino. I never go to the movies.
Niemand **will das Geschirr abwaschen.** Nobody wants to wash the dishes.
Man kann *nichts* dafür. You can't do anything about it.

Sondern

The conjuction *sondern* is used to neutralize a negative statement. It corresponds to the English "but" used in the sense of "but on the other hand" or "but rather."

Das ist kein Telefonbuch, *sondern* ein Katalog. That is not a telephone book, but a catalogue.
Ich faulenze nicht, *sondern* ich arbeite langsam! I'm not goofing off, but working slowly!
Du bist nicht nur faul, *sondern* auch frech! You are not only lazy, but impudent as well!

29. Interrogatives and Exclamations

1. The most common interrogatives in German are:

Welcher?/Welche?/Welches?	Which?	**Wieso?**	How come? Why?
Wer?	Who?	**Warum?**	Why?
Wen?	Whom? (accusative)	**Wann?**	When?
Wem?	(to) Whom? (dative)	**Wo?**	Where?
Wessen?	Whose? (genitive; rarely used)	**Woher?**	Where (do you come/are you coming) from?
Was?	What?	**Wohin?**	Where (are you going) to?
Wie?	How?		

Was gibt es zum Essen?	What are we having to eat?
Wohin willst du morgen?	Where do you want to go tomorrow?
Wieso willst du nichts essen?	How come you don't want to eat anything?
Woher kommt das Fleisch?	Where does this meat come from?

Note: Only *welcher* and *wer* are inflected for case. For the inflection of *welcher*, see *kein/keine* on page 92.

2. German has a number of "flavor" words that cannot always be translated readily into English.

doch!	yes, of course (used to counteract a negative statement)
Er ist gestern nicht nach Hause gekommen.	He did not come home yesterday.
Doch! **Er ist** *doch* **nach Hause gekommen.**	Yes, he did (too)! He *did* come home.
ja!	really (used for emphasis)
Es ist *ja* **kalt!**	It really is cold!
aber!	(is it) ever (used for emphasis)
Mensch, ist es aber kalt!	Man, is it ever cold!
denn!	(well) then (used to indicate impatience)
Wie heißt du *denn?*	What, then, is your name?
Was ist *denn* **das?**	What on earth is that?
gerade	right now (conveys immediacy)
Was machen Sie *gerade?*	What are you doing right now?
nur, bloß	only, just
Das Buch kostet *nur (bloß)* **fünf Dollar!**	The book costs only (just) five dollars!
Denken Sie nur, es kostet *bloß (nur)* **fünf Dollar!**	Just think, it costs only (just) five dollars!

30. Practical Sentence Rules

Sentence Types

There are three basic kinds of sentences in German, all described in terms of the position of the inflected verb. There are two "main sentence" or "main clause" types (*Hauptsatz/Hauptsätze*) and one "subordinate sentence" or "subordinate clause" type *(Nebensatz/Nebensätze)*.

Main Sentences/Clauses

1. The *Hauptsätze* include the statement *(Aussagesatz)*, the question *(Fragesatz)*, and the imperative *(Befehl)* sentence. In a statement, the subject usually comes first. The conjugated verb is, however, *always* the second element in the sentence.

Ich *komme* nach Hause.	I am coming home.
Der Student *schreibt* einen Aufsatz.	The student is writing a composition.
Mathias und Anna *haben* vorige Woche geheiratet.	Matthew and Ann got married last week.
Wir *möchten* jetzt gehen.	We would like to go now.

2. Often in German some element other than the subject is placed first in the sentence. The conjugated verb is *still* the second element.

So etwas *habe* ich oft gesagt.	I have often said things like that.
Meiner Großmutter *schreibt* unser Vater jetzt einen Brief.	Our father is writing my grandmother a letter right now.
Wenn ich eine Million Dollar hätte, *würde* ich mir ein großes Haus bauen lassen.	If I had a million dollars, I would have a big house built.

3. In a question, the conjugated verb is placed *first* in the sentence if the question is a "yes/no" *(ja/nein)* question. If it is not a "yes/no" question, the verb is placed directly after the question word (*Was? Wer? Wen? Wem? Wo? Wann? Warum?* etc.).

Willst du mit uns gehen?	Do you want to go with us?
Hat er dich gesehen?	Did he see you?
Sehen wir uns nächste Woche?	Will we see each other next week?
Was *machst* du gerade?	What are you doing right now?
Wann *kommt* er nach Hause?	When is he coming home?
Warum *müssen* wir diese Prüfung machen?	Why do we have to do this exam?

4. In commands, the imperative form of the verb comes first.

Kommen Sie **sofort!**	Come immediately!
Macht **eure Hausaufgaben!**	Do your homework!
Sag **das bitte nicht!**	Please don't say that!

Subordinate Sentences/Clauses

Nebensätze include all clauses that begin with a so-called *subordinating conjunction.* Subordinating conjunctions include 1) all relative pronouns, 2) all question-words used in an indirect statement ("He didn't tell us, *when* he was coming."), and 3) the following words:

daß	that	**da**	since, because
wenn	if, whenever	**seit (dem)**	since
weil	because	**nachdem**	after
als ob	as if	**während**	while
obwohl	although	**auch wenn**	even if
als	when (single event in the past)		

Ich weiß nicht, *wann* **er zu uns kommen** *wird.*	I don't know, when he will come over (to our house).
Er hat uns gestern geschrieben, *daß* **er erst übermorgen abreisen** *kann.*	He wrote us yesterday, that he cannot leave until the day after tomorrow.
Er ist der Onkel, *den* **du vorigen Sommer in Chicago kennengelernt** *hast.*	He is the uncle (whom) you met last summer in Chicago.

Second Position, Last Position

The conjugated verb is always second in a statement or a question beginning with a question-word. It is first in "yes/no" questions. It is last in subordinate clauses. If the verb has a *complement,* such as a separable prefix or an infinitive, that element comes *last* in the given clause, except where the conjugated verb would come last.

Wir *fangen* **pünktlich um neun Uhr** *an.*	We begin promptly at nine o'clock.
Er hat soeben gesagt, daß wir pünktlich um neun Uhr *anfangen.*	He just said, that we begin promptly at nine o'clock.
Ich *möchte* **gerne eine Tasse Kaffee mit Milch** *bestellen.*	I would like to order a cup of coffee with milk.
Ich wiederhole, daß ich gerne eine Tasse Kaffee mit Milch *bestellen möchte!*	I repeat, that I would like to order a cup of coffee with milk!
Die Schüler *haben* **ihre Hausaufgaben sehr schön** *gemacht.*	The pupils (students) did their homework very nicely.
Der Lehrer war immer sehr froh, wenn die Schüler ihre Hausaufgaben sehr schön *gemacht haben.*	The teacher was always very happy, when (ever) the pupils did their homework very nicely.

Time, Manner, Place

1. Expressions of time come before expressions of place. This is the exact opposite of what happens in English.

Ich komme um fünf Uhr nach Hause.	I'm coming home at five o'clock.
Wir haben uns vorige Woche in Boston kennengelernt.	We met in Boston last week.

2. If expressions of time, manner, and place were to be found in the same sentence, the line up would be time, manner, place.

Wir fahren sonntags gern auf das Land.	We enjoy driving to the country on Sundays.

31. Suffixes

A number of suffixes carry special meanings. The most common are:

-t/-en found on all past participles

-er -er (a male who performs some action)
der Arbeiter worker

-in -er, -ess (a female who peforms some action)
die Arbeiterin worker

-ung -ing (an abstraction of an action)
die Übung exercising, exercise
die Täuschung illusion
die Befreiung liberation, freeing

-heit/-keit -hood, -ty
die Schönheit beauty
die Einheit unit, unity
die Feuchtigkeit humidity
die Mannigfaltigkeit variety

-(")e -ness (the quality of something)
die Güte goodness, quality
das Richtige that which is correct, right
die Treue faithfulness

-ieren a verb suffix of French origin found in many foreign verbs
studieren study
diskutieren discuss
konsultieren consult
regulieren regulate

-schaft -ship
die Freundschaft friendship

-bar -ble
eßbar edible
machbar feasible
furchtbar terrible
annehmbar acceptable
ausdehnbar expandable

-tum -dom
der Reichtum wealth
das Irrtum error

-los -less ("without")
kinderlos childless
furchtlos fearless
machtlos powerless
glaslos without glass
arbeitslos without work, unemployed

-ig -y
ruhig quiet, quietly

-isch -y
typisch typical

-ei -y
die Partei (political) party

-ie -y
die Harmonie harmony

-erei -ry
die Bäckerei bakery
die Molkerei dairy
die Gießerei foundry

The suffix -erei is frequently attached to the stem of a verb to make fun of the activity in question.

die Lauferei (useless) running around
die Fragerei asking (foolish) questions
die Fliegerei flying around (all the time!)

32. Time

Times of the Day

der Tag, -e   day, days
täglich   daily
Tages-   daily (*used in compound words, such as* Tageszeitung, *"daily newspaper."*)
der Vormittag   morning, forenoon
der Nachmittag   afternoon

der Mittag   noontime (*not necessarily 12:00 p.m.*)
die Nacht, Nächte   night, nights
die Mitternacht   midnight
der Abend, -e   evening, evenings

Days of the Week

die Woche, -n   week, weeks
wöchentlich   weekly
Wochen-   weekly (*used in compound words, such as* Wochenzeitschrift, *"weekly magazine."*)
der Montag   Monday
der Dienstag   Tuesday
der Mittwoch   Wednesday
der Donnerstag   Thursday
der Freitag   Friday
der Samstag   Saturday
(der Sonnabend)   (*Alternate term for "Saturday" in the North and East of Germany*)
der Sonntag   Sunday

am (an dem) Freitag   on Friday
am Dienstag   on Tuesday
am Mittwoch   on Wednesday
jeden Sonntag   every Sunday
jeden Donnerstag   every Thursday
jeden Samstag   every Saturday
nächsten Sonntag   next Sunday
letzten Donnerstag   last Thursday
vorigen Samstag   last (*the previous*) Saturday
montags   Mondays, every Monday
mittwochs   Wednesdays, every Wednesday
freitags   Fridays, every Friday

Months

der Monat, -e   month, months
monatlich   monthly
Monats-   monthly (*used in compound words, such as* Monatskarte, *"monthly ticket."*)
der Januar   January
(der Jänner)   (*Alternate term for "January" in Austria*)
der Februar   February
(der Feber)   (*Alternate term for "February" in Austria*)

der März   March
der April   April
der Mai   May
der Juni   June
der Juli   July
der August   August
der September   September
der Oktober   October
der November   November
der Dezember   December

Seasons

im (in dem) Mai   in May
im Oktober   in October
jeden Februar   every February
jeden März   every March
nächsten April   next April
die Jahreszeit, -en   season, seasons
der Frühling   spring
der Sommer   summer
der Herbst   autumn

der Winter   winter
im Herbst   in (the) autumn, fall
im Frühling   in (the) spring
jeden Sommer   every summer
jeden Winter   every winter
nächsten Winter   next winter
letzten Frühling   last spring
vorigen Herbst   last (*the previous*) autumn

The Year

das Jahr, -e   year, years
jedes Jahr   every year
jährlich   yearly, annual
Jahres-   yearly, annual (*used in compound words, such as* Jahresbericht, *"annual report."*)

das Jahrhundert, -e   century, centuries
das Jahrzehnt, -e   decade, decades
das Jahrtausend, -e   millenium, millenia

Telling Time

Wieviel Uhr ist es? *or* Wie spät ist es?	What time is it?
Es ist 9.34 Uhr. (neun Uhr vierunddreißig.)	It is 9:34.
Es ist 8.15 Uhr. (acht Uhr fünfzehn./ Viertel nach acht./Viertel neun.*)	It is 8:15./a quarter past eight.
Es ist 7.30 Uhr. (sieben Uhr dreißig./ halb acht.*).	It is 7:30.
Es ist 6.45 Uhr. (sechs Uhr fünfundvierzig./Viertel vor sieben./ Dreiviertel sieben.*)	It is 6:45./a quarter to seven.

*Note: Telling time at a quarter, half, and three-quarters *before* the next hour are expressions commonly heard in the South. However, they are becoming common in other parts of the German-speaking world as well.

Telling time according to a 24-hour clock is the method used for all official time expressions, such as those found in railroad stations, airports, radio broadcasts, television programs, and university schedules. However, the 24-hour method of telling time does not use expressions such as *Viertel nach* or *Dreiviertel vor.* Only the hour followed by the minutes is used.

Die Zeit beim Gongschlag ist 21.10 Uhr (einundzwanzig Uhr zehn).	The time at the tone is 9:10 p.m.
Die Vorlesung beginnt um 13.30 Uhr (dreizehn Uhr dreißig).	The lecture begins at 1:30 p.m.

Dates

Heute is Freitag, der fünfte Mai neunzehnhundertvierundachtzig (der 5. Mai 1984).	Today is Friday, the fifth of May 1984.
Heute haben wir Freitag, den fünften Mai 1984 (den 5. Mai 1984).	Today is the fifth of May 1984.
Mein Geburtstag ist am siebenundzwanigsten April (am 27. April).	My birthday is on the twenty-seventh of April.
Mein vierzigster Geburtstag war am Freitag, dem 27. April 1984.	My 40th birthday was on Friday, April 27, 1984.

Other Time Expressions

ab und zu   now and then
damalig-   at that time (*adjective*)
damals   at that time (*in the past*)
dann   then
gelegentlich   occasionally
gestern   yesterday
gestern abend   yesterday evening
gestrig-   yesterday (*adjective*)
häufig   frequently
heute   today
heute früh   this morning
heute abend   this evening, tonight
heute nacht   last night
heutig-   today (*adjective*)
immer   always
jetzig-   now, the present (*adjective*)
jetzt   now
manchmal   sometimes
morgen   tomorrow
morgen früh   tomorrow morning

morgig-   tomorrow (*adjective*)
nie   never
oft   often
selten   rarely
übermorgen   the day after tomorrow
vorgestern   the day before yesterday
das Mal, -e   time, times (*point in time*)
die Zeit, -en   time, times (*span of time*)
einmal (ig-)   once (one time)
zweimal (ig-)   twice (two times)
dreimal (ig-)   three times
zehnmal   ten times
hundertvierzigmal   140 times
das erste Mal   the first time
zum ersten Mal   for the first time
das zehnte Mal   the tenth time
zum zehnten Mal   for the tenth time
das letzte Mal   the last time
zum letzten Mal   for the last time
das nächste Mal   the next time

33. Vocabulary Lists

Territorial Divisions

das Land, Länder land, country, rural area
die Stadt, Städte city, urban area
die Hauptstadt, Hauptstädte capital
die Gemeinde, -n community
der Bezirk, -e district
der Bund, Bünde federation

das Bundesland, Bundesländer state (*in Germany and Austria*)
der Bundesstaat, -en state (in the USA)
der (Land) Kreis, -e "(land) circle" (*equivalent of American county*)

The German-Speaking Countries

die Bundesrepublik Deutschland (Westdeutschland) the Federal Republic of Germany (West Germany)
die Deutsche Demokratische Republik (Ostdeutschland) the German Democratic Republic (East Germany)
das Fürstentum Liechtenstein the Principality of Liechtenstein

die Republik Österreich (Österreich) the Republic of Austria (Austria)
die Schweizerische Eidgenossenschaft (die Schweiz) the Swiss Confederation (Switzerland)

Commonly Used Words and Phrases

Everyday Greetings and Expressions

Grüß Gott! Hello! (*in the South*)
Gute Nacht! Good night!
Guten Abend! Good evening!
Guten Tag! Hello! Good day!
Servus! Hello! (*in the South; also* "Good-bye"*)
Ade! Good-bye! (*in the South*)
Auf Wiederhören! Good-bye! (*on radio or telephone*)
Auf Wiederschauen! Good-bye!
Auf Wiedersehen! Good-bye!
Tschüß Good-bye! (*colloquial*)
Auf Ihr/dein/euer Wohl! To your health!
Pros(i)t! Cheers!
Zum Wohl! To your health!
Guten Appetit! "Bon appetit!"
Laß es Ihnen/dir/euch schmecken! "Bon appetit!" (*formal*)

Mahlzeit! "Bon appetit!" (*colloquial*)
Ich (wir) gratuliere(n)! Congratulations!
Kommen Sie/komm/kommt gut nach Hause! Arrive home safely!
Gute Fahrt/Reise! Have a pleasant trip! "Bon voyage!"
Viel Glück! Good luck!
Viel Erfolg! Good luck! Hope you're successful!
Hals- und Beinbruch! Break a leg!
Toi, toi, toi! Good luck!
Angenehme Ruhe! Sleep well!
Viel Vergnügen! Have a good time!
Achtung! (Auf die Plätze!) Ready! (On your mark!)
Fertig! Get set!
Los! Go!

Responses

Ja Yes
Nein No
Vielleicht Perhaps
Doch! Yes, definitely (*contradicts negatives*)
Natürlich!
Selbstverständlich!
Sicher! } Of course!
Freilich!
Das kommt darauf an. That depends.
Das geht Sie/dich/euch nichts an! That is none of your business!
Bitte? What was that? Please repeat.
Bitte
Bitte sehr } Please. Here you are. You're welcome.
Bitte schön
Quatsch!
Unsinn! } Nonsense!
Blödsinn!
Gleichfalls
Ihnen/dir/euch auch } Same to you

Na und? So what?
Ach ja? Oh, really?
Also! So! Now then! As I was saying...
Aufpassen! Be careful! Watch out!
Vorsicht! Be careful!
Meinetwegen As far as I'm concerned
Entschuldigung! Excuse me! (*to get someone's attention*)
Verzeihung! Pardon me! (*to ask forgiveness*)
Danke
Vielen Dank } Thank you
Danke vielmals
Wieso? How come?
Also gut! All right, it's decided!
(Aber) Trotzdem... (But) Just the same...
Ruhe! Silence! Be quiet!
Hilfe! Help!

The Family

die Familie, -n family

die (Ur) (Groß) Eltern (great) (grand) parents
der (Ehe) Mann, (Ehe) Männer husband
die (Ehe) Frau, -en wife
der Großväter grandfather
die Großmutter, Großmütter grandmother
der Urgroßvater, Urgroßväter great grandfather
die Urgroßmutter, Urgroßmütter great grandmother
der Onkel, - uncle
die Tante, -n aunt
das Kind, -er child
der Sohn, Söhne son

die Tochter, Töchter daughter
der Bruder, Brüder brother
die Schwester, -n sister
der Schwager, -* brother-in-law
die Schwägerin, -nen* sister-in-law
der Vetter, -n cousin (*masc.*)
die Kusine, -n cousin (*fem.*)
der Neffe, -n nephew
die Nichte, -n niece
der (Ur) Enkel, - (great) grandson
die (Ur) Enkelin, -nen (great) granddaughter
der Verwandte, -n relative (*masc.*)
(ein Verwandter)
die Verwandte, -n relative (*fem.*)

***Note:** The prefix *Schwieger-* means "-in-law" for other relatives, for example *Schwiegersohn*, "son-in-law."

Characteristics (*Nouns*)

die Eigenschaft, -en characteristic

das Alter age
die Armut poverty
die Aufregung excitement
das Böse the bad, the evil
die Breite, -n width
die Dummheit, -en stupidity
die Entfernung, -n distance
das Falsche the false
die Faulheit laziness
die Feindseligkeit hostility
der Fleiß industriousness
die Freundschaft friendship
der Frieden peace
das Gewicht, -e weight
die Größe, -n size
die Güte goodness, quality
das Gute the good

die Härte, -n hardness
die Höhe height
die Jugend youth
die Länge, -n length
die Langeweile boredom
die Lüge, -n lie
der Reichtum wealth
das Richtige the correct
die Schwäche, -n weakness
die Schwierigkeit, -en difficulty
die Stärke, -n strength
die Schönheit, -en beauty
die Spannung tension
die Treue faithfulness
der Wahnsinn insanity
die Wahrheit truth
die Weisheit wisdom

Characteristics (*Adjectives*)

alt old
aufgeregt excited
aufregend exciting, stirring
billig cheap
böse angry, bad, evil
doof stupid (*colloquial*)
dumm dumb, stupid
einfach easy
falsch false, wrong
faul lazy
feindlich hostile
fleißig industrious, hard-working
friedlich peace-loving
freundlich friendly
früh early
gespannt eager, thrilled, excited
gut good
hart hard
häßlich ugly
intelligent intelligent
interessant interesting
jung young
klug intelligent, smart
langweilig boring
laut loud, noisy
leicht light, easy
leise quiet
lieb dear, nice
nah near
nett nice

neu new
preiswert inexpensive
pünktlich on time, punctual
rauh rough
rechtzeitig in time
reich rich
roh raw
ruhig peaceful, quiet
sanft smooth, soft (*surface*)
schlecht bad
schlimm bad, unfortunate
schön fine, beautiful, nice, good
schlau clever
schwer heavy
schwierig difficult
spannend exciting, suspenseful, absorbing
spät late
teuer expensive
treu faithful
uralt ancient, very old
verrückt crazy, insane
wahnsinnig insane
wahr true
wild wild
weich soft (*texture*)
weise wise
weit far
zeitig very early, ahead of time

Color

die Farbe, -n   color

blau blue	**schwarz** black
braun brown	**weiß** white
gelb yellow	**dunkel** dark
grün green	**grell** bright, loud (*color*)
grau gray	**hell** light
rot red	

Size

die Größe, -n   size

breit wide	**kurz** short
dick fat, thick	**niedrig** low
dünn thin	**riesig** giant
eng narrow	**schwach** weak
groß big, great, large, tall (*persons*)	**stark** strong
hoch high, tall (*objects*)	**tief** deep
klein small, little	**winzig** tiny
lang long	

The Weather (*Nouns*)

das Wetter   weather

die Bewölkung cloudiness, overcast conditions	**die Kälte** cold
der Dunst haze	**der Nebel** fog
die Feuchtigkeit humidity	**der Regen** rain
der Gefrierpunkt the freezing point	**der Schnee** snow
der Grad (*Celsius*) degree (*Celsius*)	**der Siedepunkt** the boiling point
der Hagel hail	**die Temperatur, -en** temperature
die Hitze heat	**die Wärme** warmth
	die Wolke, -n cloud

The Weather (*Adjectives*)

bewölkt cloudy	**kühl** cool
dunstig hazy	**nebelig** foggy
feucht humid	**regnerisch** rainy
frisch fresh, brisk	**schwül** muggy
heiß hot	**trüb** hazy, foggy, overcast
heiter bright and sunny	**warm** warm
kalt cold	**wolkig** cloudy
klar clear	

Everyday Objects

der Gegenstand, Gegenstände object

der Bericht, -e report
der Bleistift, -e pencil
der Bleistiftspitzer, - pencil sharpener
der Brief, -e letter *(correspondence)*
die Briefmarke, -n postage stamp
das Buch, Bucher book
der Buchstabe, -n letter of the
alphabet
das Heft, -e notebook, notepad
die Kreide chalk
der Kugelschreiber, - ballpoint pen
der Kuli, -s ballpoint pen *(colloquial)*

die Mine, -n ballpoint pen refill
cartridge
das Papier, -e paper *(the material or documents)*
der Radiergummi, -s eraser
das Referat, -e (term) paper
der Schwamm, Schwamme
blackboard eraser, sponge
der Stempel, - rubber stamp
die Tinte ink
der Umschlag, Umschlage envelope

The House

das Haus, Häuser house

der Ausgang exit
das Badezimmer, - bath
der Eingang entrance
das Eßzimmer, - dining room
der Fußboden, Fußböden floor of
a room
der Gang, Gänge corridor, aisle
die Garage, - garage
der Garten, Gärten garden, yard

die Küche, -n kitchen
die Mauer, -n wall *(freestanding)*
der Rasen lawn
das Schlafzimmer, - bedroom
das Schloß, Schlösser lock
der Schlüssel, - key
die Tür, -en door
das Wohnzimmer, - living room

The Room

das Zimmer, - room

das (Bücher) Regal, -e bookcase
die Bude, -n very small room
die Decke, -n ceiling, blanket
die Ecke, -n corner
das Fenster, - window
die Gardine, -n curtain
der Hocker, - stool
die Lampe, -n lamp
das Möbel, - furniture
der Raum, Räume large room
der Regalboden, Regalböden shelf
der Schrank, Schränke cupboard,
cabinet, closet

der Schreibtisch, -e desk
das Sofa, -s sofa
der Spiegel, - mirror
die Stube, -n small room
der Stuhl, Stühle chair
der Teppich, -e rug
die Uhr, -en clock, watch, timepiece
der Vorhang, Vorhänge drape,
curtain
die Wand, Wände wall *(inside a building)*

The Bed

das Bett, -en bed

der Bettlaken, - sheet
das Bettuch, Bettücher sheet
die Decke, -en blanket

das Kissen, - pillow
die Matraze, -n mattress

The Table

der Tisch, -e   table

das Besteck silverware	**das Öl** oil
der Essig vinegar	**das Pfeffer** pepper
die Gabel, -n fork	**die Platte, -n** platter
das Geschirr plates, cup, saucers, pots, pans, etc.	**das Salz** salt
das Glas, Gläser glass	**die Serviette, -n** napkin
der Krug, Krüge pitcher, beer mug ("Stein")	**die Tasse, -n** cup
	der Teller, - plate
der Löffel, - spoon	**die Tischdecke, -n** table cloth
das Messer, - knife	**die Untertasse, -n** saucer
	der Zucker sugar

Beverages

das Getränk, -e   beverage

das Bier beer	**der Most** cider
der Kaffee coffee	**der Saft, Säfte** juice
der Kakao cocoa	**der Tee** tea
die Limonade, -n soft drink	**das Wasser** water
die Milch milk	**der Wein** wine

Meat

das Fleisch   meat

der Braten, - roast	**der Schinken, -** ham
das Hammelfleisch mutton	**das Schnitzel, -** cutlet, tenderloin
das Kotlett, -en cutlet, chop	**das Schweineflesch** pork
das Kalbfleisch veal	**der Speck** bacon
das Lammfleisch lamb	**die Wurst, Würste** sausage
das Rindfleisch beef	

Poultry

das Geflügel   poultry, fowl

die Ente, -n duck	**der Pute, -n** turkey
die Gans, Gänse goose	**der Truthahn, Truthähne** turkey
das Huhn, Hühner chicken	

Fish

der Fisch, -e   fish

der Aal, -e eel	**der Karpfen, -** carp
die Forelle, -n trout	**der Lachs, -e** salmon
der Kabeljau cod	

Vegetables

das Gemüse vegetables

der **Blumenkohl** cauliflower
die **Bohne, -n** bean
die **Erbse, -n** pea
die **Gurke, -n** cucumber, pickle
die **Karotte, -n** carrot
die **Kartoffel, -n** potato
der **Knoblauch** garlic
der **Kohl** cabbage
der **Kürbis, -e** squash, pumpkin

die **Linse, -n** lentil
die **Möhre, -n** carrot
die **Olive, -n** olive
der **Rettich, -e** raddish
der **Rosenkohl** brussels sprouts
der **Salat** lettuce (*also,* salad)
der **Schnittlauch** chives
die **Tomate, -n** tomato
die **Zwiebel, -n** onion

Grain

das Getreide cereal grains

die **Gerste** barley
der **Mais** corn
der **Reis** rice

die **Rogge** rye
der **Weizen** wheat

Fruits

das Obst fruits

die **Ananas, -** pineapple
der **Apfel, Äpfel** apple
die **Aprikose, -n** apricot
die **Banane, -n** banana
die **Birne, -n** pear
die **Dattel, -n** date
die **Erdbeere, -n** strawberry
die **Feige, -n** fig
die **Himbeere, -n** raspberry
die **Johannisbeere, -n** currant

die **Kirsche, -n** cherry
die **Limone, -n** lime
die **Melone, -n** melon
die **Orange, -n** orange
der **Pfirsich, -e** peach
die **Pflaume, -n** plum
die **Preiselbeere, -n** cranberry
die **Stachelbeere, -n** gooseberry
die **Traube, -n** grape
die **Zitrone, -n** lemon

Food and Meals

die **Mahlzeit, -en** meal time
die **Nahrung** food, nourishment

das **Abendbrot** supper
das **Abendessen** dinner
die **Beilage, -n** side dish, side order
das **Brot** bread
das **Brötchen, -** roll
die **Butter** butter
das **Ei, -er** egg
der **Eintopf** stew
das **Eis** ice, ice cream
die **Erfrischung** refreshment
das **Essen** food
das **Frühstück** breakfast
das **Gebäck** pastry, baked goods
das **Gericht, -e** meal, "dish"
das **Hauptgericht, -e** main dish

der **Honig** honey
der **Imbiß** snack
der **Käse** cheese
der **Kuchen, -** cake
die **Marmelade** marmelade
das **Mittagessen** lunch
der **Nachtisch** dessert
der **Salat, -e** salad
der **Senf** mustard
die **Soße, -n** sauce
die **Speise, -n** meal, food
die **Speisekarte, -n** menu
die **Suppe, -n** soup
die **Torte, -n** pie, pastry

Animals

das Tier, -e   animal

der Bär, -en bear	**die Kuh, Kühe** cow
der Bulle, -n breed bull	**das Kätzchen, -** kitten
das Eichhörnchen, - squirrel	**der Löwe, -n** lion
der Fuchs, Füchse fox	**die Maus, Mäuse** mouse
der Hase, -n hare	**das Pferd, -e** horse
der Hengst, -e stallion	**die Ratte, -n** rat
der Hund, -e dog	**die Schildkröte, -n** turtle
die Hundin, -nen female dog	**die Schlange, -n** snake
das Kalb, Kälber calf	**der Stier, -e** bull
das Kaninchen, - rabbit	**die Stute, -n** mare
die Katze, -n cat	**der Wolf, Wölfe** wolf
der Kater, - male cat, tom cat	**der Wurm, Würmer** worm

Birds

der Vogel, Vögel   bird

der Adler, - eagle	**der Papagei, -en** parrot
der Eichelhäher, - blue jay	**die Schwalbe, -n** swallow
die Elster, -n magpie	**der Sittich, -e** parakeet
der Hahn, Hähne rooster, cock	**der Spatz, -en** sparrow
die Henne, -n hen	**der Specht, -e** woodpecker
das Kücken, - chick	**die Taube, -n** pigeon, dove

Insects

das Insekt, -e   insect

die Ameise, -n ant	**die Motte, -n** moth
die Biene, -n bee	**die Mücke, -n** mosquito
die Fliege, -n fly	**der Schmetterling, -e** butterfly
der Floh, Flöhe flea	**die Spinne, -n** spider
die Heuschrecke, -n grasshopper	

Trees

der Baum, Bäume   tree

der Ahorn maple	**die Linde, -n** linden
der Ast, Äste (large) branch	**die Palme, -n** palm
der (Baum)Stamm, (Baum)Stämme trunk, log	**die Papel, -n** poplar
die Eiche, -n oak	**die Tanne, -n** fir, spruce
die Rinde bark	**der (Wal) Nußbaum, (Wal)Nußbäume** walnut
die Kastanie, -n chestnut	**die Wurzel, -n** root
die Kiefer, -n spruce	**der Zweig, -e** (small) branch, twig

Plants and Flowers

die Pflanze, -n plant

die Blume, -n flower
die Blumenzwiebel, -n flower bulb
die Blüte, -n blossom
das Blatt, Blätter leaf
das Blütenblatt, Blütenblätter petal
der Flieder lilac
die Gänseblume, -n daisy
das Gras grass

die Lilie, -n lily
der Löwenzahn dandelion
das Maiglöckchen, - lily of the valley
die Nelke, -n carnation
die Rose, -n rose
die Tulpe, -n tulip
das Veilchen, - violet

The Earth

die Erde earth, soil, ground

die Atmosphäre atmosphere
der Bach, Bäche stream
der Berg, -e mountain
der Boden, Böden floor, bottom, ground
die Bucht, -en bay
das Feld, -er field
der Fluß, Flüsse river
das Gebirge, - mountain range
der Golf, -e gulf
die Halbinsel, -n peninsula
der Himmel sky
die Höhle, -n cave
der Hügel, - hill
die Insel, -n island
das Kap, -s cape

der Kontinent, -en continent
die Küste, -n coast
die Landschaft landscape, scenery
die Luft air
das Meer, -e sea, ocean
der See, -n lake
der Strand, Strände beach
der Sumpf, Sümpfe swamp, marsh
das Tal, Täler valley
der Teich, -e pond
das Ufer, - shore
der Wald, Wälder forest
der Weiher, - fish pond
die Wiese, -n meadow
die Wüste, -n desert

The City

die Stadt, Städte city

die Großstadt, Großstädte city *(over 100,000 population)*
die Kleinstadt, Kleinstädte town *(under 100,000 population)*
die Allee, -n avenue
die Ampel, -n traffic light
die Bank, Bänke bench
die Bank, -en bank
die Bibliothek, -en library
der Bürgersteig, -e sidewalk
der Dom, -e cathedral
das Dorf, Dörfer village
die Fabrik, -en factory
der Friedhof, Friedhöfe cemetery
die Gasse, -n alley (street, *in Austria*)
der Gehsteig, -e sidewalk
die Gemeinde, -n community, municipality

der Hafen, Häfen port, harbor
das Kino, -s movie theater
die Kirche, -n church
das Krankenhaus, Krankenhäuser hospital
das Museum, Museen museum
der Park, -s park
der Pfad, -e path
der Platz, Plätze square
das Rathaus, Rathäuser city hall
die Rennbahn, -en race track
das Schild, -er traffic sign
das Stadion, Stadien stadium
die Straße, -n street
das Theater, - theater
der Weg, -e way

Shopping

das Geschäft, -e business, store
der Laden, Läden shop, store

die Apotheke, -n pharmacy,
  drugstore
die Bäckerei, -en bakery
die Bar, -s cocktail lounge
die Buchhandlung, -en bookstore
das Cafe, -s cafe
die Drogerie, -n drugstore (without
  drugs)
die Einkaufstasche, -n shopping bag
die Gaststätte, -n restaurant
das Kaufhaus, Kaufhäuser
  department store

die Kneipe, -n bar
die Konditorei, -en pastry shop
der Markt, Märkte market
die Metzgerei, -en butcher shop
das Restaurant, -s restaurant
die Reinigung dry cleaning
der Supermarkt, Supermärkte
  supermarket
die Tüte, -n paper bag
die Wäscherei, -en laundry

Transportation

der Verkehr traffic

die Ausfahrt, -en exit
das Auto, -s car
die Autobahn, -en freeway
das Autobahnkreuz, -e freeway
  interchange
das Boot, -e boat
der Bus, -e bus
der Dampfer, - steamer
die Einfahrt, -en entrance
die (Eisen)Bahn, -en railway
das Fahrrad, Fahrräder bicycle
das Fahrzeug, -e vehicle
der Flughafen, -häfen airport
das Flugzeug, -e airplane
der Fußänger, - pedestrian
die Fußängerzone, -n pedestrian mall
das Kreuz, -e cross, crossing
die Kreuzung, -en crossing, junction

der Lastwagen, - truck
der LKW, -s* truck
die Maschine, -n (commercial)
  airplane
das Motorrad, Motorräder
  motorcycle
der PKW, -s* passenger vehicle, car
die S-Bahn rapid transit
das Schiff, -e ship
das Segelboot, -e sailboat
die Spur, -en traffic land
die Straßenbahn, -en streetcar, tram
das Taxi, -s taxi
die U-Bahn underground, subway
der Verkehrsstau, -s traffic jam
der Wagen, - car
die Zufahrt, -en approach

*Note: LKW = *Lastkraftwagen,* PKW = *Personenkraftwagen*

Travel

die Reise, -n   trip, journey, travel

die Abfahrt, -en   departure
die Ankunft, Ankünfte   arrival
der Aufzug, Aufzüge   elevator
der Bahnhof, -höfe   railroad station
der Bahnsteig, -e   platform
die Fahrkarte, -n   ticket
die Fahrt, -en   trip, drive
der Fahrplan, Fahrpläne   travel
schedule, time table
der Fensterplatz, Fensterplätze
window seat
der Gangplatz, Gangplätze   aisle seat
das Gepäck   baggage, luggage
der Gepäckträger, -   porter
das Gleis, -e   track

das Hotel, -s   hotel
die Jugendherberge, -n   youth hostel
der Koffer, -   suitcase
der Liegewagen, -   sleeping car
die Lokomotive, -n   locomotive
die Reisetasche, -n   travel bag
der Schaffner, -   conductor
der Schalter, -   (ticket) window
der Schlafwagen, -   sleeping car,
pullman
die Sehenswürdigkeit, -en   sight
(something worth seeing)
der (Sitz)Platz, (Sitz)Plätze   seat
der Speisewagen, -   dining car
der Zug, Züge   train

The Human Body

der Körper, -   body

die Ader, -n   artery
der Arm, -e   arm
das Auge, -n   eye
die Backe, -n   cheek
die Bandscheibe, -n   vertebra
der Bauch, Bäuche   abdomen, belly
die Bauchspeicheldrüse, -n   pancreas
das Bein, -e   leg
die Blase, -n   bladder
die Brust, Brüste   chest, breast
die Drüse, -n   gland
der Finger, -   finger
der Fuß, Füsse   foot
das Fußgelenk, -e   ankle
das Gehirn   brain
das Haar, -e   hair
der Hals, Hälse   neck
die Hand, Hände   hand
das Handgelenk, -e   wrist
die Haut, Häute   skin
das Herz, -en   heart
der Kiefer, -   jaw
das Kinn, -e   chin
das Knie, -   knee

der Knochen, -   bone
der Kopf, Köpfe   head
die Kopfhaut   scalp
der Kreislauf   circulatory system
die Leber, -n   liver
die Lippe, -n   lip
die Lunge, -n   lung
der Magen, Mägen   stomach
die Milz, -en   spleen
der Nagel, Nägel   nail
der Mund, Münder   mouth
die Nase, -n   nose
der Nerv, -en   nerve
die Niere, -n   kidney
das Ohr, -en   ear
der Rücken, -   back
die Schulter, -n   shoulder
die Stirn, -en   forehead
die Vene, -n   vein
die Wange, -n   cheek
die Wirbelsäule, -n   spinal column
der Zahn, Zähne   teeth
die Zehe, -n   toe
die Zunge, -n   tongue

Clothing

die Kleidung   clothing

die Armbanduhr, -en wristwatch	**der Schuh, -e** shoe
der Ärmel, - sleeve	**die Schürze, -n** apron
das Badetuch, Badetücher bath towel	**die Socke, -n** sock
die Bluse, -n blouse	**der Stiefel, -** boot
die Handtasche, -n handbag, purse	**der Strumpf, Strümpfe** stockings
das Handtuch, Handtücher towel	**die Tasche, -n** bag, sack, pocket,
das Hemd, -en shirt	purse, pouch
die Hose, -n pair of trousers	**das Taschentuch, Taschentücher**
das Kleid, -er dress	handkerchief
der Kragen, - collar	**die Taschenuhr, -en** pocket watch
die Krawatte, -n tie	**die Unterwäsche** underwear
der Rock, Röcke skirt	**die Wäsche** laundry

Professions

die Arbeit   work

der Beruf, -e   profession

der (Rechts)Anwalt, (Rechts)Anwälte
die (Rechts)Anwältin, -nen } lawyer

der Architekt, -en
die Architektin, -nen } architect

der Arzt, Ärzte
die Ärztin, -nen } physician

die (Erz)Bischof, (Erz)Bischöfe (arch)bishop

der Fotograf, -en
die Fotografin, -nen } photographer

der Geistliche, -n   clergyman

der Imam, -e *(islamisch)*   imam *(Islamic)*

der Kardinal, Kardinäle   cardinal

der Lehrer, -
die Lehrerin, -nen } teacher

der Matrose, -n   sailor

der Musiker, -
die Musikerin, -nen } musician

der Papist, Päpste   pope

der Pfarrer, - *(evangelisch)*   minister *(Protestant, Lutheran)*

der Pilot, -en
die Pilotin, -nen } pilot

der Polizist, -en
die Polizistin, -nen } police officer

der Priester, - *(katholisch)*   priest *(Catholic)*

der Rabbiner, - *(jüdisch)*   rabbi *(Jewish)*

der Schauspieler, -
die Schauspielerin, -nen } actor

die Schreibkraft, Schreibkräfte   file clerk

der Sekretär, -en
die Sekretärin, -nen } secretary

der Soldat, -en   soldier

der Zahnarzt, Zahnärzte
die Zahnärztin, -nen } dentist

Education

der Abschluß degree, completion of studies
die Abschlußklausur, -en final examination
die Ausbildung professional training
die Bildung learning, culture, education
das Diplom, -e diploma *(in natural sciences)*
der Doktor(grad) doctorate
die Erziehung education, teaching
das Examen, - examination
die Hochschule, -n university
die Klausur, -en (in-class) test
der Magister(grad) masters

die Prüfung, -en test, examination
die Schule, -n school
der Schüler, - pupil *(primary or secondary)*
die Schülerin, -nen
der Student, -en student *(university only)*
die Studentin, -nen
das Studium, Studien academic study
der Stundenplan, Stundenpläne schedule, time table
die Universität, -en university
das Vorlesungsverzeichnis, -se university catalogue

Academic Subjects

das Fach, Fächer subject
das Hauptfach, Hauptfächer major subject
das Nebenfach, Nebenfächer minor subject

(die) Amerikanistik American studies
(die) Anglistik English language and literature
(die) Biologie biology
(die) Erziehungswissenschaften education
(die) Fremdsprache, -n foreign language
(die) Geisteswissenschaft, -en humanities
(die) Germanistik German language and literature
(die) Geschichte history
(die) Informatik information or computer sciences

(die) Ingenieurwissenschaften engineering
(die) Mathematik mathematics
(die) Naturwissenschaft, -en natural sciences
(die) Philosophie philosophy
(die) Physik physics
(die) Romanistik Romance languages and literatures
(die) Theologie theology
(die) Wirtschaftswissenschaften economics

Titles

der Titel, - titel

die Anrede, -n forms of address
(der) Herr, -en Mr., Lord, sir
(die) Frau, -en Mrs., Ms., woman, lady
der Präsident, -en president
Herr Präsident Mr. President
die Präsidentin, -nen president
Frau Präsidentin Madame President
der Professor, -en ⎫
die Professorin, -nen ⎬ professor

Herr Professor Professor *(man)*
Frau Professor Professor *(woman)*
der Doktor, -en Ph.D., Doctor of philosophy. *(any doctorate)*
Herr Doktor Doctor *(man)*
Frau Doktor Doctor *(woman)*
der Minister, - ⎫
die Ministerin, -nen ⎬ minister (of state)
Herr Minister Mister Minister
Frau Ministerin Madame Minister

Units of Measurement

das Maß, Masse   measurement

der *or* **das Liter, -**   liter
das *or* **der Meter, -**   meter
das Gramm,-   gram
das Kilo(gramm), -   kilo(gram)
das Pfund, -   one-half kilogram, 500 grams

das *or* **der Kilometer, -**   kilometer
das Hektar, -   hectare
der Zoll, -   inch
der Fuß, -   foot
die Gallone, -n   gallon
die Tonne, -n   (metric) ton

Geometry

die Geometrie   geometry

der Winkel, -   angle
der rechte Winkel, -   right angle
das Rechteck, -e   square
das Viereck, -e   rectangle
das Dreieck, -   triangle
der Kreis, -e   circle
der Halbkreis, -e   semicircle
der Durchmesser   diameter
der Radius/Halbmesser   radius

die Linie, -n   line
der Rhombus   rhombus
der Würfel, -   cube
die Kegel, -n   cone
die Kugel, -n   sphere
die Halbkugel, -n   hemisphere
die Pyramide, -n   pyrimid
das Prisma, Prismen   prism

Chemistry

die Chemie   chemistry

das Element, -e   element
die Flüssigkeit, -en   liquid
das Gas, -e   gas
das Metall, -e   metal
das Blei   lead
das Eisen   iron
das Gold   gold

der Kohlenstoff   carbon
das Kupfer   copper
der Sauerstoff   oxygen
das Silber   silver
der Stickstoff   nitrogen
der Wasserstoff   hydrogen
das Zinn   tin

Materials

der Backstein   brick
die Baumwolle   cotton
der Beton   concrete
der Gips   plaster
das Glas   glass
der Gummi   rubber
das Holz   wood
der Kalkstein   limestone
die Keramik   ceramic
der Kunststoff   plastic

der Marmor   marble
das Metall   metal
das Plastik   plastic
die Seide   silk
der Stahl   steel
der Stein   stone
der Stoff, -e   material, fabric
der Stuk   stucco
die Wolle   wool
der Ziegel   tile

Holidays and Holiday Greetings

der Feiertag, -e holiday
das Fest, -e festival
die Feier, -n celebration
die Ferien (plural) holidays, vacation
der Urlaub vacation
Frohe Festtage! Happy Holidays!
(das) Weihnachten* Christmas
(der) Heilige Abend Christmas Eve
Frohe Weihnachten! Merry
 Christmas!
Fröhliche Weihnachten!
(das) Neujahr New Year's Day
Gutes Neues Jahr! Happy New Year!
(der) Sylvester New Year's Eve
(das) Ostern* Easter

Frohe Ostern! Happy Easter!
(das) Pfingsten* Pentecost
(der) Heilige(r) Sankt Nikolaus Saint
 Nicholas' Day *(December 6)*
(die Heilige(n) Drei Könige Epiphany
 (January 6)
(der) Rosenmontag Monday before
 Ash Wednesday
(der) Faschingsdienstag Tuesday
 before Ash Wednesday
(der) Aschermittwoch Ash
 Wednesday
(der) Gründonnerstag Holy Thursday
(der) Karfreitag Good Friday

*Note: *Weihnachten, Ostern,* and *Pfingsten* usually appear in the plural, as in *Frohe Weihnachten,* or in compounds, such as *Ostersonntag* ("Easter Sunday") or *Pfingstwoche* ("Week of Pentecost").

Abbreviations

die Abkürzung, -en abbreviation

AG Aktiengesellschaft (stock) corporation
Betr. Betreff/betrifft re, regarding
bzw. beziehungsweise or (respectively)
Fa. Firma _____ _____Company
Fam. Familie _____ (Mr. and Mrs.) _____ and family
Fr. Frau Mrs., Ms.
Frl. Fräulein Miss
GmbH Gesellschaft mit beschränkter Haftung (limited liability) corporation, Ltd.
Hr(n). Herr(n) Mr.
i. R. im Ruhestand retired
Nr. Nummer number, No.
PLZ Postleitzahl postal code, ZIP Code
usw. und so weiter and so on, etc.
vgl. vergleiche compare, cf.
z. B. zum Beispiel for example, e.g.
z. Z. zur Zeit at present

Index

LANGUAGE AND REFERENCE BOOKS

Dictionaries and References
VOX Spanish and English Dictionaries
Cervantes-Walls Spanish and English Dictionary
Klett German and English Dictionary
NTC's New College French & English Dictionary
NTC's New College Greek & English Dictionary
Zanichelli New College Italian & English Dictionary
Zanichelli Super-Mini Italian & English Dictionary
NTC's Dictionary of Spanish False Cognates
NTC's Dictionary of German False Cognates
NTC's Dictionary of *Faux Amis*
NTC's American Idioms Dictionary
NTC's Dictionary of American Slang and
 Colloquial Expressions
Forbidden American English
Essential American Idioms
Contemporary American Slang
Everyday American English Dictionary
Everyday American Phrases in Content
Beginner's Dictionary of American English Usage
NTC's Dictionary of Grammar Terminology
Robin Hyman's Dictionary of Quotations
Guide to Better English Spelling
303 Dumb Spelling Mistakes
NTC's Dictionary of Literary Terms
The Writer's Handbook
Diccionario Inglés
El Diccionario Básico Norteamericano
British/American Language Dictionary
The French-Speaking World
The Spanish-Speaking World
Guide to Spanish Idioms
Guide to German Idioms
Guide to French Idioms
101 Japanese Idioms
Au courant
Guide to Correspondence in Spanish
Guide to Correspondence in French
Español para los Hispanos
Business Russian
Yes! You Can Learn a Foreign Language
Japanese in Plain English
Korean in Plain English
Easy Chinese Phrasebook and Dictionary
Japan Today!
Everything Japanese
Easy Hiragana
Easy Katakana
Easy Kana Workbook
The Wiedza Powszechna Compact Polish & English
 Dictionary

Picture Dictionaries
English; French; Spanish; German

Let's Learn...Picture Dictionaries
English, Spanish, French, German, Italian

Verb References
Complete Handbook of Spanish Verbs
Complete Handbook of Russian Verbs
Spanish Verb Drills
French Verb Drills
German Verb Drills

Grammar References
Spanish Verbs and Essentials of Grammar
Nice 'n Easy Spanish Grammar
French Verbs and Essentials of Grammar
Real French
Nice 'n Easy French Grammar
German Verbs and Essentials of Grammar
Nice 'n Easy German Grammar
Italian Verbs and Essentials of Grammar
Essentials of Russian Grammar
Essentials of English Grammar
Roots of the Russian Language
Reading and Translating Contemporary Russian
Essentials of Latin Grammar
Swedish Verbs and Essentials of Grammar

Welcome to...Books
Spain, France, Ancient Greece, Ancient Rome

Language Programs: Audio and Video
Just Listen 'n Learn: Spanish, French, Italian, German,
 Greek
Just Listen 'n Learn PLUS: Spanish, French, German
Speak French
Speak Spanish
Speak German
Practice & Improve Your...Spanish, French, Italian,
 German
Practice & Improve Your...Spanish PLUS, French PLUS,
 Italian PLUS, German PLUS
Improve Your...Spanish, French, Italian, German: The
 P & I Method
Conversational...in 7 Days: Spanish, French, German,
 Italian, Portuguese, Greek, Russian, Japanese, Thai
Everyday Japanese
Japanese for Children
Nissan's Business Japanese
Contemporary Business Japanese
Basic French Conversation
Basic Spanish Conversation
Everyday Hebrew
VideoPassport in French and Spanish
How to Pronounce Russian Correctly
How to Pronounce Spanish Correctly
How to Pronounce French Correctly
How to Pronounce Italian Correctly
How to Pronounce Japanese Correctly
L'Express: Ainsi va la France
L'Express: Aujourd'hui la France
Der Spiegel: Aktuelle Themen in der Bundesrepublik
 Deutschland
Listen and Say It Right in English
Once Upon a Time in Spanish, French, German
Let's Sing & Learn in French & Spanish

"Just Enough" Phrase Books
Chinese, Dutch, French, German, Greek, Hebrew,
 Hungarian, Italian, Japanese, Portuguese, Russian,
 Scandinavian, Serbo-Croat, Spanish
Business French, Business German, Business Spanish

Language Game and Humor Books
Easy French Vocabulary Games
Easy French Crossword Puzzles
Easy French Word Games and Puzzles
Easy French Grammar Puzzles
Easy Spanish Word Power Games
Easy Spanish Crossword Puzzles
Easy Spanish Vocabulary Puzzles
Easy French Word Games and Puzzles
Easy French Culture Games
Easy German Crossword Puzzles
Easy Italian Crossword Puzzles
Let's Learn about Series: Italy, France, Germany, Spain,
 America
Let's Learn Coloring Books in Spanish, French, German,
 Italian, English
Let's Learn...Spanish, French, German, Italian, English
 Coloring Book-Audiocassette Package
My World in...Coloring Books: Spanish, French,
 German, Italian
German à la Cartoon
Spanish à la Cartoon
French à la Cartoon
101 American English Idioms
El alfabeto
L'alphabet

Getting Started Books
Introductory language books in Spanish, French,
 German, Italian

Ticket to...Series
France, Germany, Spain, Italy (Guide and audiocassette)

Getting to Know...Series
France, Germany, Spain, Italy,
 Mexico, United States

PASSPORT BOOKS
a division of *NTC Publishing Group*
Lincolnwood, Illinois USA